## Other Books by the Author

### RAISING CAIN
*The Life and Politics of Senator Harry P. Cain*

### COMMUNITY GODFATHER
*How Sam Volpentest Shaped the History
of Hanford and the Tri-Cities*

# In the Wake

## *of*

# Lewis and Clark

### From the Mountains to the Sea

C. Mark Smith

ISBN: 978-1-4834-2839-0 (sc)
ISBN: 978-1-4834-2838-3 (e)

Because of the dynamic nature of the Internet, any web addresses or links contained in this book may have changed since publication and may no longer be valid. The views expressed in this work are solely those of the author and do not necessarily reflect the views of the publisher, and the publisher hereby disclaims any responsibility for them.

Any people depicted in stock imagery provided by Thinkstock are models, and such images are being used for illustrative purposes only. Certain stock imagery © Thinkstock.

Lulu Publishing Services rev. date: 03/20/2015

Dedication

To those who went before
and made all things possible

# Contents

# Introduction and Acknowledgments

A VAST LIBRARY of books has been written about Lewis and Clark and the Corps of Discovery. It includes histories, biographies of the participants, letters and journals, detailed maps, books of campfire recipes, books about the birds, fish, and animals the explorers encountered, books about the trees and plants they discovered, and books for cyclists, canoeists, and campers who want to follow their trail. The majority of these books, but certainly not all, are listed in the bibliography of this book.

I have my particular favorites, which I drew on heavily in order to write this book. Bernard DeVoto's 1952 classic, *The Course of Empire*, is an important place to start. Among contemporary works, I believe Stephen Ambrose's 1996 *Undaunted Courage* is perhaps the best one-volume history of the expedition. I can particularly recommend Emory and Ruth Strong's *Seeking Western Waters: The Lewis and Clark Trail from the Rockies to the Pacific*, published in 1995 by the Oregon Historical Society after the deaths of the Strongs. Their 1980s manuscript provides a vivid day-by-day description of the expedition during its time in the Pacific Northwest, along with excellent editing by Herbert K. Beals and many wonderful photographs from the archives of the Oregon Historical Society.

Dayton Duncan and Ken Burns published a lively text full of beautiful and informative pictures for their companion book for the PBS television series, *Lewis and Clark*. My friend David Nicandri, historian and former director of the Washington State Historical Society, helped me in immeasurable ways when I wrote my first two books, and he has helped me once again with his 2009 book, *River of Promise: Lewis and Clark on the Columbia*. Barbara Fifer and Vicky

Soderberg published *Along the Trail with Lewis and Clark*, which provides historical highlights, excellent color maps, and information about where to stay and what to do if you want to follow the path of the Corps of Discovery.

I have personally traveled the route of Lewis and Clark down the Columbia River and back many times, but the computer has enhanced that experience. Following the route on Google Maps allows the viewer to follow the place names and points of interest from a different perspective. Following the route using Google Earth allows you to see multi-dimensional birds-eye views. But none of these efforts to trace the expedition are meaningful without being able to refer to the historical accounts of those who were there.

The definitive work in this regard is Gary E. Moulton's thirteen-volume work, *The Journals of the Lewis and Clark Expedition*, published by the University of Nebraska Press between 1983 and 2001. For the first time, all the surviving journals (and we know we don't have them all) have been compiled in one place, using a standard format and extensive detailed footnotes. In addition, some of the diarists revised their journal entries in the field or after they returned back to the United States.

While Lewis and Clark were both educated men, Lewis was the more educated, and his prose shows it. Clark spent much of his life on the frontier, and his writing reflects that fact. However unorthodox his spelling, punctuation, and grammar, it doesn't keep him from producing a vivid and often compelling narrative. When I have quoted from the journals, I have repeated the language as it appears in Moulton, enclosed in quotation marks, rather than note each inconsistency with the customary "*sic*."

This book is unlike the others I have mentioned. They are recommended if the reader wants detailed information about the expedition. What I have attempted to do with this volume is provide a concise description of Lewis and Clark's passage down the Clearwater, Snake, and Columbia Rivers and their return. It can be read by passengers aboard the American Express cruise ship and used as a reference as they pass the same places the Corps of Discovery visited in1805–1806. The book is meant to supplement the information provided by the cruise ship company's onboard "Riverlorian" and serves as an inexpensive memento of the trip.

I am indebted to James Palmeri of Shore Excursions of America for thinking of this idea and choosing me to implement it. I also want to express my appreciation to Tara Pegasus, a talented vocalist, musician, and copyeditor for improving the text. All other errors of omission or commission are mine alone.

C. Mark Smith
Richland, Washington
July 2014

# Clash of Empires

THE SEVEN YEARS' War—known as the French and Indian War to Americans—was the first truly global conflict. It was fought between 1756–1763 on the battlefields of Europe, in the backwoods of North America, on islands in the Caribbean, in Central America, along the West African coast, in India, and in the Philippines.

The war was just the latest in a series of wars between the European empires during the eighteenth century that was driven by the struggle for power and influence in Europe and the growing competition for trade and new colonies in the rest of the world. Prussia and her allies were in competition with Austria for control of what remained of the Holy Roman Empire. Great Britain competed with France and Spain for new overseas territories, untapped resources, and strategic control of key choke points around the world's oceans.

Power and influence ebbed and flowed as Europe's great monarchies sought a new balance of power. Newly emerging Prussia formed an alliance with Great Britain. They were joined by several smaller German states and, later, Portugal. In North America, the great Iroquois Confederacy fought on behalf of the British, while the Huron and other tribes allied with the French. Traditional enemies France and Austria countered with their own alliance, which was joined by Sweden, Saxony, and, later, Spain. Russia started out as Austria's ally but later signed a separate peace treaty with Prussia. In India, the Mughal Empire allied with the French.

The results of the Seven Years' War generally favored the British, who gained most of New France in Canada as a result of General James Wolfe's 1759 defeat of the French army under Montcalm on the Plains of Abraham above Quebec City. They also gained Spanish Florida, several islands in the Caribbean, and the colony of Senegal on the West African coast, and forced the French out of India. Spain lost Florida but gained the vast French holdings in Louisiana while regaining Cuba and the Philippines, which had been captured by the British during the war. The cost of undertaking a war on such a vast scale nearly bankrupted the various antagonists.

*North America after the Treaty of Paris, 1763*

In North America, none of the great powers had any real knowledge of the vast Louisiana Territory. For centuries, great powers' sea captains had searched both coasts of the continent looking for a "Northwest Passage" to the Orient. Over time the search had extended to North America. The seventeenth-century French explorers Marquette, Hennepin, and LaSalle suggested that there was a single mountain chain somewhere in the western interior beyond which a great river flowed to the Pacific Ocean.

Britain's North American colonies fought alongside the mother country, particularly against the French-backed Indian tribes in the north and west. However, after the expense of protecting its colonies, the British government felt that its increasingly prosperous colonies should pay for their own defense. The British made the decision to recover some of their costs by imposing a series of taxes, including one that taxed every document or newspaper used or printed in America. The colonists were outraged that they were being taxed without representation in Parliament, a violation, they felt, of their rights and liberties. The taxes were met by acts of civil disobedience and growing calls for independence.

By 1767, events had escalated to the point where the British government imposed a tax on all goods imported to the American colonies, and the colonists responded by boycotting British imports and halving their trade with the mother country. Not surprisingly, King George III and his government regarded the colonists' actions as insurrection and sent troops to Boston to restore the status quo.

The British government seriously underestimated the power of the American independence movement, particularly among the colonies' leading political and intellectual leaders. The charged atmosphere could not last, and, by 1774, Great Britain and its American colonies were at war. The Americans formally declared their independence two years later. Despite hired German mercenaries and the largest overseas deployment by its naval and land forces in history, the British were never able to apply enough military force or political willpower to win the war. They could defeat the Americans in battle, but they couldn't control the countryside that sustained and nurtured their foe.

By 1778, the French saw an opportunity to strike back at the British for their losses during the Seven Years' War and signed an alliance with the new government of the United States. The arrival of French land and naval forces added a new dimension to the war, making it more difficult for the British to reinforce their forces and providing the pivotal margin of victory in the decisive Battle of Yorktown, Virginia, in 1781. Within six months, the British prime minister resigned, and a peace treaty was signed in Paris in September 1783.

*North America after the Treaty of Paris, 1783*

Financial crises at home and the success of the Americans in creating their republic only increased the ambitions of those who wanted to reform the government of France. The state of the country's finances and Louis XVI's inconclusive and high-handed attempts to deal with the radical reformers led to the overthrow of the French monarchy in 1789. The events in France led Europe's other conservative monarchies—primarily Austria and Prussia—to form a coalition aimed at restoring the French monarchy. Revolutionary France then declared war on Austria and Prussia in 1792, and on Great Britain in 1793. The French and the British remained at war more or less continuously until 1814.

The young United States of America tried to stay out of the European conflict while profiting from trading with both sides. Both France and Great Britain tried to prohibit America from trading with the other side. With no real navy to protect them, American merchant ships were routinely stopped and searched, particularly by the British, and their seamen—many of whom had been born in Great Britain—were removed and impressed to fill the ranks of the Royal Navy.

Spain had claimed the Pacific coast of California as early as 1542, but other priorities in the New World meant that California would remain an imperial backwater until 1765 when Spain learned that Russians were settling in northern California. By then, Spain was fully engaged in the Seven Years' War but decided to colonize the province of Alta California with Franciscan monks protected by troops stationed at their missions.

Spanish claims to Alaska and the west coast of North America dated to the papal bull of 1493, which created the demarcation line between Spain and Portugal in the New World. Spain's claim was reinforced in 1513 when Vasco Núñez de Balboa claimed all lands adjoining the Pacific Ocean for Spain.

In 1579, British adventurer Francis Drake sailed up the west coast of North America, perhaps as far as British Columbia, before returning south to repair his ship in what is now called San Francisco Bay. There, he claimed the region for Great Britain, naming it New Albion. Around 1592, a Greek explorer employed by Spain, Juan de Fuca, was supposed to have discovered the strait of water, now named for him, separating Vancouver Island from the Olympic Peninsula of Washington state. In the 1740s, Danish explorer Vitus Bering—then in the employ of Elizabeth, empress of Russia and daughter of Peter the Great—explored Alaska and the Pacific coast, leading to Russia's claim to that region and the eventual settlements in northern California that would so alarm the Spanish.

Beginning at about the same time as the American Revolution, Spain actively explored the coastline of what is now Canada and Alaska in order to counter the Russian and British threats and strengthen its own claim. They found that vast quantities of fine fur pelts that were available for trade from the local Indian tribes. On August 17, 1775, a Spanish sea captain named Bruno de Heceta sighted the mouth of the Columbia River but could not tell if it was a river or a strait between several bodies of land. Unable to enter because of the strong currents, he named it Bahia de la Asunción.

During the next ten years the Spanish accelerated their exploration of the region and established a trading post at Nootka Sound. They soon controlled the fur trade between Asia and North America. In 1778, Captain James Cook of the British Royal Navy visited Nootka Sound, and it was not long before the British and Americans were intent on competing with the Spanish for the increasingly profitable trade.

In 1788, an American trader, Captain Robert Gray of Boston, discovered a large river at approximately 46° latitude but was unable to enter it because of the adverse tides and currents. He proceeded north to Nootka Sound, where he was joined by a second American and several British trading ships. The Spanish Navy had dispatched a warship to Nootka to enforce Spanish sovereignty and impounded the three British ships it found there.

The two American ships were left alone because Spain had been allied with France and the United States during the recent American Revolution. When news of the capture of the British ships arrived back in England, it almost led to war between Great Britain and Spain. The Nootka Convention of 1790 allowed both countries the right to settle along the Pacific coast, interrupting Spain's expansion in the New World for the first time in more than two centuries.

In May 1792, Robert Gray was finally successful in sailing into the Columbia River in his ship, the *Columbia Rediviva*, becoming the first recorded non-Native American to do so. That voyage became the basis for the US claim on the Pacific Northwest, and the river was afterward named for Gray's ship.

Later that same year, Royal Navy Lieutenant William Broughton, in the service of Captain George Vancouver, entered the Columbia in his ship, *Chatham*, and rowed up the river in the ship's boats as far as the current town of Washougal on the Washington side. His charts eventually found their way into an American map prepared for the Lewis and Clark expedition. It is quite possible—even probable—that Jefferson did not believe that Gray's discovery of the Columbia established a clear claim to the region on behalf of the United States and that the Lewis and Clark expedition was expressly designed to strengthen that claim.

While Great Britain, Spain, and the United States competed for the Pacific Northwest and the fur trade with China, momentous events were taking place in the heartland of the North American continent. France had controlled this vast area—which included the entire drainage system of the Mississippi River, from the Appalachian to the Rocky Mountains—from 1699 until 1762.

As negotiations to end the Seven Years' War began, Louis XV of France secretly proposed to his cousin, Charles III of Spain, that France give Louisiana to Spain. The agreement was kept secret even during the negotiation and signing of the Treaty of Paris, which ended the Seven Years' War in 1763. The Treaty of Paris divided La Louisiane—as the vast territory was known in French—in half, with the Mississippi River as the dividing line. As a result of Great Britain's victory in the Seven Years' War, the half of the territory located east of the Mississippi was given to it, while the western half, including New Orleans, was nominally retained by France, which had already secretly promised it to Spain.

Spain would only control its remote and unruly territory for thirty-six years. By 1800, Napoleon Bonaparte had become first consul of France. He dreamed of establishing a new French empire in the Caribbean and Louisiana. In another secret treaty, in which he gave the king of Spain's son-in-law control over the province of Tuscany in Italy, Spain agreed to return Louisiana to France.

Thomas Jefferson, who had once served as minister to France and secretary of state before being elected as the third president of the United States, was a Renaissance man who spoke five languages, understood geopolitics, and had a strategic vision of the future of the United States. In the spring of 1801, Jefferson learned of the secret treaty between Spain and France. Alarmed, he let the French know that the United States would consider any stationing of French troops in Louisiana to be an act of war.

In Jefferson's mind, so long as Louisiana remained a part of the dying Spanish empire, the United States could bide its time. The control of Louisiana by the active and aggressive Napoleon was another matter entirely. Control of the territory by the British represented the greatest threat of all.

In May 1793, a Scottish fur trader named Alexander Mackenzie, working for the British North West Company, set out from Montreal for the Pacific Ocean with a small party. He crossed the Continental Divide and reached the headwaters of the Frazier River, but when told that it was unnavigable and occupied by hostile Indians, he selected another route to the coast. Mackenzie's exploration was of immense importance to the Americans. He believed that he had discovered the northern fork of what would come to be called the Columbia River, and the publication of his journal established the British claim to the region.

Jefferson had long been interested in the west. He knew the approximate location of the mouth of the Columbia River from Gray's discovery. When Mackenzie's journal was published in London in 1801, Jefferson quickly acquired a copy of it. Mackenzie wrote that "the way to the Pacific lay open and easy," and it prompted Jefferson to take action.

He sent Robert R. Livingston to Paris to inquire about purchasing New Orleans and its immediate environs from France. Negotiations languished while Napoleon's armies were forced from Egypt and tried unsuccessfully to put down a slave revolt in Haiti. Desperate to avoid a possible war with France, Jefferson sent James Monroe to Paris in 1802 to help Livingston negotiate a settlement, with instructions to negotiate an alliance with Great Britain if the talks in Paris failed.

Jefferson had authorized Livingston to purchase New Orleans and its immediate environs at a cost not to exceed $10 million. At first Napoleon was uninterested, but his recent losses and the need to rearm in order to continue the war with Great Britain forced him to reconsider. The American negotiators were shocked when the French offered them New Orleans and all of the Louisiana Territory for only $15 million. The American negotiators accepted the French offer—hoping that Jefferson and the American congress would concur—on April 30, 1803. The treaty was quickly signed by Jefferson and ratified by Congress in October 1803.

*Louisiana Purchase, 1803*

France officially turned over the Louisiana Territory to the United States at a formal ceremony conducted in St. Louis on March 10, 1804. The Louisiana Purchase roughly doubled the physical size of the United States, adding 828,000 square miles at a cost of $11,250,000 in cash plus the assumption of an additional $3,750,000 of private American debt—approximately four cents per acre—and set the stage for the Lewis and Clark expedition.

CHAPTER ONE

# Corps of Discovery

THOMAS JEFFERSON WAS inaugurated as president of the United States on March 4, 1801. At the time, two out of three Americans lived within fifty miles of the Atlantic Ocean, and only four roads crossed the Allegheny Mountains to the west. Jefferson's young nation ended at the eastern bank of the Mississippi River, but his vision reached far beyond to the Pacific Ocean.

Aware of the many demands that would be placed on him by his new office, Jefferson decided to hire a private secretary. The man he selected was Captain Meriwether Lewis, the twenty-seven-year old son of longtime Virginia acquaintances, and a young man Jefferson had known since birth. Lewis had grown up with a love for the outdoors and a lifelong interest in natural history. He briefly served in the Army in 1794–1795, during the Whiskey Rebellion tax protest in western Pennsylvania, under an officer named William Clark.

Lewis joined Jefferson—a widower—and eleven servants who lived in the newly completed White House. There he was the president's almost constant companion. The two men pored over every page of Sir Alexander Mackenzie's journal describing his expedition to the Pacific in 1793. Concerned that the British would reach the Columbia first, and fearing that they had already done just that, Jefferson decided to mount his own expedition to the Pacific, and in the fall of 1802, decided that Lewis should lead it.

Almost immediately, Jefferson began a crash course to educate his protégé in the liberal arts, the geography of North America, botany, mineralogy, astronomy, and ethnology. At Jefferson's library at his home in Monticello, Lewis read British explorer James Cook's account of his 1776–1779 voyage to the Pacific Northwest and a history of Louisiana that had been published in 1762.

Lewis began to make preliminary plans for the trip, developing lists of supplies and expenses—including $696 for "Indian presents"—which finally totaled $2,500. Among the "Indian presents" that were purchased was a large quantity of Jefferson "peace and friendship" medals, in three sizes, to be given to Indian chiefs of various degrees of importance. The medals had a likeness of Thomas Jefferson on one side and a crossed peace pipe and tomahawk on the other. Several of these medals have since been recovered from Indian graves and are now exhibited in various museums in the Pacific Northwest.

*Jefferson Peace Medal.*
*Credit: Jefferson National Expansion Memorial*

In January 1803, Jefferson sent his funding request for the expedition to Congress in a secret message. It passed easily because, as Jefferson had planned, it represented a mere pittance compared with the more than $11 million he had just a week before asked Congress for to purchase Louisiana.

Jefferson dispatched Lewis to Philadelphia, then the center of advanced learning in America, for more training under some of America's most eminent scientists. There he also had to involve himself in the countless practical details related to provisions, equipment, and manpower that needed to be decided on. Lewis hoped to be able to depart for the west in the summer of 1803, but there were new delays involving the design and construction of a special keelboat, the purchase of scientific instruments, the selection of medicines, and other details.

Jefferson formalized the goals of the expedition in a set of written orders to Lewis:

> The object of your mission is to explore the Missouri river, & such principal stream of it, as, by its course and communication with the waters of the Pacific ocean, whether the Columbia, Oregan, Colorado or any other river that may offer the most direct & practicable water communication across this continent, for the purposes of commerce.[1]

Good maps would be essential to the development of whatever commercial activity might follow the completion of the expedition. Jefferson ordered Lewis to make careful "observations of latitude and longitude at all remarkable points on the river." He also provided guidance on what to do if confronted by a superior Indian force determined to block their progress. "You must decline it's further pursuit, and return. In the loss of yourselves, we should lose also the information you will have acquired."[2]

Jefferson hoped that when the expedition reached the Pacific Ocean, the expedition would be able to make contact with a trading ship whose captain might be persuaded to bring them back to the United States. To facilitate this, or any other eventuality, Jefferson provided Lewis with what amounted to an unlimited letter of credit on the US government, asking "Consuls, agents, merchants & citizens of any nation . . . to furnish you with those supplies which your necessities may call for."[3]

---

[1] http://www.nps.gov/lewi/historyculture/journey.htm. Original spelling has been retained.

[2] http://www.monticello.org/site/jefferson/jeffersons-instructions-to-meriwether-lewis

[3] http://jeffersonpapers.princeton.edu/selected-documents/meriwether-lewis

As Lewis proceeded with his detailed planning, he came to believe that he would need another trusted officer to accompany him on the trip. He knew just the right man. Thirty-four-year-old William Clark had been born in Virginia but spent most of his life on the Kentucky frontier. He had been Lewis's company commander when they served together during the Whiskey Rebellion, and the two men had formed a close bond.

Jefferson approved Lewis's request for a second officer on June 19, 1803. Lewis wrote to Clark (then living in Clarksville, Indiana Territory, across the Ohio River from Louisville, Kentucky) describing the mission and the planning that had occurred to date, and making him the offer of a lifetime. "If therefore there is anything under those circumstances . . . which would induce you to participate with me . . . there is no man on earth with whom I should feel equal pleasure in sharing them with yourself."[4]

On July 4, 1803—the twenty-seventh anniversary of the founding of the new nation—Jefferson announced the signing of the formal agreement to purchase Louisiana. Lewis immediately left Washington City for Pittsburgh, where the keelboat he had ordered was supposed to be completed. On July 29 word arrived that William Clark had accepted his invitation. However, in Pittsburgh on August 5, Lewis found out that only half of the boat had been planked and that the Ohio River was dropping daily. The fifty-five foot keelboat—which could be rowed or sailed, pushed by men with long poles, or pulled by men or horses on a riverbank—wasn't completed until August 31. Frantic to proceed, Lewis had it loaded and departed downriver on the same day, making his first entry into what would become the journals of Lewis and Clark.

The low waters of the Ohio River made the first weeks of travel a nightmare, as the travelers discovered the difficulty of making headway in the large keelboat. It was a challenge that would plague them all the way to the Mandan Indian villages in North Dakota.

---

[4] http://www.in.gov/dnr/lewis-clark/falls/

Lewis decided on the first day that he needed to double the number of men in the party.

He purchased several "pirogues" (large, flat-bottomed rowboats with masts), to help lighten the load in the keelboat, which kept running aground on the riverbanks or sandbars. The delays caused Lewis to abandon his hope of getting up the Missouri River before winter. He wrote to Jefferson saying that he planned to winter outside St. Louis and perhaps conduct a midwinter exploration toward Santa Fe. Fearful of alarming the Spanish, Jefferson quickly wrote back, telling Lewis to focus on his original goals.

Lewis arrived at Clarksville, where William Clark joined the party on October 15. Together, they began selecting the first members of the expedition from the local garrison. In addition to the new recruits, they were accompanied by York, Clark's slave and lifelong companion, and also Lewis's dog, Seaman.

Eleven days later they arrived at Fort Massac, located about thirty-five miles upstream from where the Ohio flows into the Mississippi River, where they signed up more recruits. On November 20, the expedition turned north and headed up the Mississippi toward St. Louis.

St. Louis was just forty years old when Lewis and Clark arrived there in 1803. It boasted a population of just more than 1,000—mostly French Canadians—and was the center of the fur trade for a huge inland region that used the Missouri River as its principal highway. Because the secret transfer of the territory from Spain to France was not yet known there, the town was still administered by the Spanish, who refused Lewis permission to travel up the Missouri. Lewis was unconcerned, because he knew what Jefferson knew and realized that he would have to winter in the vicinity.

The party set up their winter camp on the Illinois side of the river, across from the mouth of the Missouri. The winter was difficult—hard on discipline with the combination of inactivity and nearby whiskey sellers. However, the already prosperous St. Louis merchants were certainly happy to see them arrive. Lewis set about buying necessary supplies, including all the wooden barrels he could find, a small bronze cannon, and several flintlock blunderbusses, which he mounted on swivels on the keelboat. More voyagers were hired to paddle the pirogues so that the core of soldiers could remain together on the keelboat.

On March 10, 1804, Lewis was present at the ceremony marking the formal transfer of Louisiana from Spain to France, and then from France to the United States. On May 14, they were finally on their way up the Missouri—Captains Lewis and Clark; Clark's slave, York; three sergeants; twenty-two privates; and eight hired voyagers who would return with the keelboat when the Missouri was no longer navigable.

They quickly divided their duties. Most often, Clark remained on the keelboat, while Lewis walked the shore collecting specimens, noting the geography, and looking for Indians. Occasionally, they would encounter traders returning downriver, their pirogues filled to overflowing with fur pelts.

*Painting of French soldiers firing a salute as the US flag is raised in ceremonies marking the transfer of the Louisiana Territory to the United States.*
*Credit: Library of Congress*

While Lewis and Clark exercised equal authority, their journals—and, more important, letters that Lewis sent back from the Missouri River—give the impression that Lewis was the actual commander, both because he had helped plan the expedition, and also because of his personality. Clark was the perfect executive officer. Lewis was better educated and had a better understanding of Jefferson's desires, but he was also moody, introspective, and melancholy. Clark was his perfect complement—a born frontiersman, genial, outgoing, and totally at home in the wilderness. His writing was far less refined than Lewis's, but his no-nonsense style provided a vivid picture of what he was trying to say, and he had a real genius for geography and map-making.

The Indians tended to like Clark, while Lewis remained aloof and somewhat distant. Most historians have painted a picture of complete cordiality between the two men, but historian David Nicandri, in his 2009 book, *River of Promise*, hints at a different story. He suggests that Lewis intentionally arranged events so that he would be the first to view the Great Falls of the Missouri and have an unrestricted view of the Pacific Ocean.

By late June they had traveled some 600 miles and reached the mouth of the Platte River. Each day brought new discoveries—least terns, white pelicans, coyotes, pronghorn antelope, prairie dogs, black-tailed deer, elk, and buffalo in ever-increasing numbers. Later that month they experienced their first casualty when Sergeant Charles Floyd succumbed to what Lewis described as "Biliose Chorlick." Private Patrick Gass, whose writing would become an important addition to the history of the trip, was elected to replace him.

And then, at sunset on August 2, they encountered their first Indians—a large hunting party of Osos and Missouris. Lewis and Clark invited them to parley at a site near what became known as Council Bluffs, Iowa. They began to perfect what would become their standard modus operandi for dealing with Indian tribes. They would call a council, smoke Clark's tomahawk pipe, give away some trade goods or medals to the chiefs, and enjoy a meal. Lewis would shoot his patent air gun, York would dance around with his arms out like an angry bear, and one of the men would play his violin so all could dance. Afterward, on Jefferson's orders, Lewis would try to compile a glossary of specific words he had heard.

They met their first members of the mighty Sioux confederacy near present-day Yankton, South Dakota. These Yankton Sioux were already trading with a French fur trader, George Drouillard, who provided translation for the meeting. He would later join the expedition as an interpreter. In September they found themselves in a much more difficult situation when a large party of Teton Sioux stopped them with the intention of charging a toll of guns and whiskey before they would allow the party to proceed upriver. An armed standoff ensued, and bloodshed was only averted by Lewis's hesitancy to open fire and the Sioux chief's personal intervention after some tobacco was thrown toward him on the riverbank.

As they entered what would become North Dakota, they passed through the villages of the Arikara Indians (also known as Rees). By the end of October, north of present-day Bismarck, North Dakota, they arrived at the numerous villages of the Arikaras's arch-enemies, the Mandan. Lewis knew that the Mandan Indians were at the center of the trade that took place on the Northern Plains, attracting Indians from great distances, as well as white traders from Hudson's Bay and the rival North West Company in British Canada.

The captains decided to winter with the friendly Mandans, and it was there on November 4 that they met Toussaint Charbonneau and his fifteen-year-old squaw, Sacajawea, then six months pregnant. A Shoshone (in some accounts, she is referred to as a Snake Indian), she had been captured by a war party of Hidatsas, and Charbonneau had won her release in a bet with her captors. Their recent encounters with the Sioux had proven the importance of good translators, and Lewis signed them up to join the expedition on the spot. Charbonneau turned out to be something of a disappointment, but Sacajawea quickly earned the captains' confidence by digging for artichokes and prairie turnips and picking berries and wild licorice for their dinners. She would later on more than prove her worth.

*Reconstructed Fort Mandan, North Dakota.*
*Credit: US Army*

The winter of 1804–1805 was brutally cold. The Missouri River was so frozen that large herds of buffalo could walk across it. The soldiers maintained regular military discipline but interacted in every way with the nearby Mandan, particularly the women, in their off hours. The days were filled with hunting, trading, socializing, and keeping fit. On February 11, Lewis assisted as Sacajawea gave birth to a son, named Jean Baptiste Charbonneau.

Lewis spent much of the winter catching up on his writing. As the river ice began to break up, he wrote his long-overdue report to President Jefferson. The extensive chronicle, dated April 7, 1805, combined his personal observations with first- and second-hand information he received from others. He sent back 108 botanical specimens, sixty-eight mineral specimens, the skeletal remains of numerous mammals, and even live magpies and prairie dogs. The report also included Clark's map of the United States west of the Mississippi. It was a masterpiece, highly accurate about what they had seen, but progressively less so as it described where they were headed.

The information provided by the Mandans about the Rocky Mountains and beyond came from Nez Percé Indians, who had visited the Mandan villages over the years. The Nez Percé had also traveled west, at least as far as the Great Falls of the Columbia River, so they were in a position to pass along information—however sketchy—about the western rivers and their people, which the Mandans passed on to Lewis and Cark. The captains were unclear about the original source of the information, but it found its way into their journal entries in the form of river names used in the report to Jefferson.

Later that day, April 10, Lewis sent the keelboat and the French-Canadian voyagers back down the Missouri River in the care of a sergeant and several men, while the remaining members of the Corps of Discovery got into their two pirogues and six canoes and headed up the Missouri into the unknown.

On they went, rounding the Great Bend of the Missouri and finally heading west. Past the mouths of the Yellowstone, the Milk, and the Marias Rivers, past the Great Falls of the Missouri—three hundred yards wide and eighty feet tall—which Lewis described as the "grandest sight I ever beheld."[5] On May 26, Lewis climbed a bluff and saw the Rocky Mountains for the first time.

On July 4, 1805, the men celebrated by eating a meal of beans, suet dumplings, and heaping portions of buffalo meat, "a very comfortable dinner,"[6] Lewis wrote. They also finished off the last of their whiskey. For an evening, the celebration overshadowed the fact that they were badly behind schedule. The eighteen-and-a half-mile portage around the Great Falls had taken from June 16 to July 15 to accomplish.

On July 27, the party reached a place they named Three Forks, where three rivers they named the Gallatin, Jefferson, and Madison Rivers came together to form the Missouri. The information they had received earlier from the Mandans and Hidatsas hadn't alerted them to these forks in the river, and it was imperative that they pick the right one. Lewis wrote: "Not knowing how far these mountains continue, or wher to direct our course to pass them to advantage or intercept a navigable branch of the Columbia, or even were we on such an one the probability is that we should not find any timber within these mountains large enough for canoes if we judge from the portion of them through which we have passed."

---

[5] *The Lewis and Clark Journals* (University of Nebraska, 2003), xxxiii.
[6] http://www.gutenberg.org/files/8419/8419-h/8419-h.htm

After exploring the other forks, the captains decided to proceed almost due south along the Jefferson. Their progress was slowed by the need to carve new dugout canoes to replace the pirogues left behind at the Marias and the Belt Creek, and by the failure of Lewis's pet project—an experimental metal-framed boat. They were beset by hordes of mosquitoes and numerous rattlesnakes, by prickly pear that shredded their moccasins and needle grass that penetrated their leggings and, most dangerous, by huge and aggressive grizzly bears.

The delay in picking the right fork of the river had cost them another ten days. But soon Sacajawea began to recognize portions of the river she had known as a child. As they descended, they searched in vain for the Shoshone Indians who Sacajawea had said would be there. On August 12, Lewis and his small party followed an Indian path to the head of a stream they considered to be the source of the "heretofore deemed endless Missouri."[7]

Later that day they crossed the Continental Divide at Lemhi Pass into present-day Idaho. From there, the rivers ran west, but the mountains continued on in front of them in their snow-covered and endless confusion. The tributaries of the Columbia River were still more than 250 miles to the west of them. They knew neither the route nor the distance, only that they would need help.

The next day, they continued down into the valley and finally met the elusive Shoshone Indians, whom they counted on to provide that help. They tried to approach two women and a man, but the Indians fled. Then they came across an old woman and two children who were convinced that they were about to be killed by marauding Blackfeet. Lewis gave them some gifts and calmed their fears about the same time as a large Shoshone war party arrived at full speed, alerted by the man who had run away. The woman spoke to them on Lewis's behalf, and together they proceeded to the village of the local chief, Cameahwait, who was cautious, but friendly.

Although the Shoshone feared a Blackfoot ambush, Lewis convinced them, with the help of Drouillard's sign language, to go

---

[7] http://www.gutenberg.org/files/8419/8419-h/8419-h.htm

back with him and wait until Clark brought the canoes and the rest of the party up the river. With growing difficulty, Lewis was able to stall until Clark finally arrived with Sacajawea and the rest of the party. In an almost unbelievable stroke of good fortune, it turned out that Cameahwait's band was the one from which Sacajawea had been abducted, and that she and Cameahwait were sister and brother!

From Cameahwait, Lewis learned of a path through the mountains used by small parties of Nez Percé when they traveled from their home in the west to hunt buffalo in the Missouri River country. The trail was described as very bad with little game to be had. Clark described it as a place where the mountains were "broken rockey and so thickly covered with timber that they could scarcely pass."[8] Lewis was delighted. If the Indians with their women and children could make it through that pass, his men could too.

But they would need horses. At first the Shoshone Indians were willing to sell them some for trade goods and bits of uniforms, but as the Indians better understood the party's plight, the price went up to include some of their guns, and the promise of more on their return trip. There was no other choice. It was September and winter was fast closing in. They acquired thirty-eight horses and a few mules, some in only fair condition. Cameahwait found an old man who had been over the Nez Percé trail and who was willing to guide them. The captains named him "Old Toby," and he and his two sons would guide the Corps of Discovery west for the next eight weeks.

On September 4, they encountered a band of approximately 400 Flathead (Salish) Indians, who were allies of the Shoshone, on their way east to hunt buffalo. While they are still sometimes referred to as Flatheads, the term is confusing. They did not flatten the heads of their infants as did the Chinook Indians of the lower Columbia River. Rather, the term is thought to have originated because the tops of their heads were thought to be unusually flat. These Indians spoke a language different from any they had encountered so far. Clark wrote, "we assembled the Chiefs & warriers and Spoke to them (with much

---

[8] http://www.gutenberg.org/files/8419/8419-h/8419-h.htm#link22H_4_0058

dificuely as what we Said had to pass through Several languajes before it got in to theirs, which is a gugling kind of languaje Spoken much thro the fhrought."[9] The Flatheads sold them a few more excellent horses. They would need them all.

The party camped at a place not far from today's Missoula, Montana. They called it "Travellers Rest." On September 11, they began to ascend the Bitterroot Mountains. It would be the worst ordeal they had encountered so far during the entire trip. Four days later, Clark climbed up to a vantage spot and wrote, "From this mountain I could observe high ruged mountains in every direction as far as I could See."[10] Winter was already beginning in the high country.

On September 16, it snowed six to eight inches. The men were cold, wet, and hungry. Trying to breathe in the cold mountain air, the party marched for thirteen painful miles "with great difficuelty," Clark wrote. "I have [never] been [as] wet and cold in every part . . . in my life."[11] Their provisions were almost gone, and there was no game to be had. The men's spirits were flagging, and they neared the end of their endurance. On September 18, they camped at a place Clark named Hungry Creek and ate one of their horses. It was the low point of the expedition so far. How much longer could they survive in the deepening winter?

---

[9] http://www.gutenberg.org/files/8419/8419-h/8419-h.htm#link22H_4_0058
[10] http://www.gutenberg.org/files/8419/8419-h/8419-h.htm#link22H_4_0058
[11] http://www.gutenberg.org/files/8419/8419-h/8419-h.htm#link22H_4_0058

## CHAPTER TWO

# In the Land of Twisted Hair

IN DESPERATION, CLARK decided to take six soldiers—his best hunters—and forge ahead to hunt for game. On the morning of October 18 they set out toward a valley they could see in the distance. They continued toward it for two more difficult days. On the twentieth, they descended out of the mountains and onto Weippe Prairie, not far from today's Weippe, Idaho. The prairie had long been a gathering place for Nez Percé families who came to dig Camus roots and fish in the Clearwater River. After proceeding about three miles they saw some tepees and then surprised Nez Percé children gathering roots. The children ran off, but before long an elderly man came out from the village to welcome Clark. Taken to a large lodge and provided with buffalo meat, dried berries, and roots by the elderly residents, Clark was told that the chief and all of the warriors had departed three days previously to battle with a neighboring tribe and would return in two or three weeks.

Clark sent back a soldier with some food to alert Lewis and tell him of their good fortune. When Clark's news reached him the next day, Lewis could not restrain his emotions. "The pleasure I now felt in having triumphed over the rocky Mountains and descending once more . . . can be more readily conceived than expressed." It would be the last entry Lewis would make in his journal until January 1806, while the expedition wintered over at Ft. Clatsop. Their passage over the Bitterroots had proven that there was not just one chain of mountains, but several, effectively ending the dream of a short portage over the Rocky Mountains and an easy land route to the Pacific.

Meanwhile, Clark moved on to a larger village. Here he had time to record his thoughts about his new hosts. Like the Flatheads, the Nez Percé had no previous contacts with whites and had received only a limited amount of European trade goods as a result of their contacts with the Columbia River tribes. The Nez Percé were by far the largest and most powerful tribe in the Pacific Northwest. Their name had been given to them by French-Canadian fur traders who encountered them in the late 1700s, but the name is an inaccurate description of the tribe. They did not practice nose piercing. What they did do—very well—was raise horses. They owned more horses than any other tribe in North America and had an active horse breeding program. They lived on deer and elk, supplemented by the innumerable numbers of salmon provided by the Snake and Columbia River systems. Clark was the first white person most of them had ever seen.

He described his new hosts as large and "stout likely men, handsom women, and very dressey in their way." Their language was much different from the Salish spoken by the Flatheads. Without knowing it, Clark and his small party had passed through an important linguistic boundary and were now with Indians who spoke Sahaptian. Clark recorded that they called themselves "Chopunnish or Pierced noses."

Clark's small party stayed at the village until September 21, gorging themselves on salmon and Camus root, with the captain trying to obtain as much information as he could about the rivers and country ahead. He was told that the tribe's head chief was then fishing at a river only half a day's march away. He decided to go there to meet him and hired a guide to take him "to the Camp of the twisted hare" located on a small island one mile above today's town of Orofino, Idaho.

Clark described Twisted Hair as "a Chearfull man of apparent sincerity of about sixty-five years" with whom he smoked and talked through sign language until the early hours of the morning. The Nez Percé didn't know what to do with the strangers. At first they

15

considered killing Clark and his six hunters for their guns, but according to historian Stephen Ambrose, they were dissuaded from doing so by an elderly Nez Percé woman who had been captured by the Blackfeet several years before and taken to Canada, where she had been sold to a white trader and treated well. She told the warriors, "These are the people who helped me. Do them no hurt."

However, the welcome they received was probably based on more than the word of an old woman. The Nez Percé, like their Flathead and Shoshoni neighbors, were desperate to get their hands on guns. The prospect of future trade and the hope of being able to acquire guns from the whites may have influenced Twisted Hair's treatment of the expedition more than anything else.

At the same time, Lewis was trying to round up his horses in order to join Clark below. Clark and Twisted Hair found him the next day "Encamped, much fatigued, hungery, much rejoiced to find something to eate . . . . I cautioned them of the Consequences of eating too much &c." Clark's warnings proved to be of little use because the abrupt change in diet caused most of the party, including Lewis, to come down with severe cases of dysentery. Lewis was particularly hard hit and was nearly immobilized for many days.

Clark obtained accurate information about the river route they would follow to the Columbia. A little optimistically, Twisted Hair estimated that it would take them five days to reach the Falls of the Columbia "where the white traders lived." The captains had no intention of remaining any longer than necessary among the Nez Percé, regardless of how helpful they were. Their immediate needs were to replenish their food supplies and trade in their horses for canoes.

On September 26 the party moved to a place they called "Canoe Camp" because they found timber there suitable for building the dugout canoes they would need for the rest of their journey. They fashioned four large and one small canoe from Ponderosa pine trees. The Indians had never before seen an ax, but once the trees were felled, they hollowed them out in the traditional way, using fire controlled with wet moss or mud. After the trees burned for the necessary amount of time, the fire and charcoal were removed with the help of stone adzes. Some of the men were still too sick to work, but they slowly recovered. Clark wrote, "We have nothing to eate except dried fish & roots which disagree with us verry much . . . Capt Lewis Still Sick but able to walk about a little."

On October 5 they branded their thirty-eight horses with Lewis's branding iron, which bore the legend "U.S. Capt, M. Lewis," (one of the few authenticated items to survive the expedition), and left them in the care of some of Twisted Hair's relatives. They hid their saddles and a lead canister full of powder and musket balls in a hollowed-out tree to be picked up on their return trip.

In a gesture that would have important consequences, Twisted Hair volunteered to accompany them down what he referred to as the *Kos kos-kee* River (today's Clearwater River) in order to introduce the strangers to his fellow tribesman. On October 7, with Clark now feeling the full effects of their new diet, they set out down the river.

*Site of canoe accident on the Clearwater River*
*- Oregon Historical Society*

The canyon walls squeezed the river into a narrow and seemingly never-ending series of rapids—they passed fifteen on October 8 alone. Near the entrance of the Potlatch River into the Clearwater, the pine canoe piloted by Sergeant Gass hit a rock and split open, dumping Gass and the rest of his cargo of important trade goods into the river. Old Toby, the elderly Shoshone who had guided them across the Bitterroots, was now in hostile country and so frightened of the boiling water that he left camp without receiving his pay, although he took Clark's spoon. They camped near the site of the accident, unloading their cargo and drying it out—often hampered by rain—until October 10.

On that day the expedition set out at 7 a.m. under clear skies and passed through yet another set of rapids. They passed many villages whose residents lined the river to watch them as they paddled past. One of their large canoes became stuck on a sandbank, and it took more than an hour and the help of some local Indians to dislodge it. Several hours later they reached the point where the Clearwater empties into a big bend in the Snake River from the east. They camped below the dramatic hills on the right bank of the river opposite what is now Clarksville, Washington, just downstream from Lewiston, Idaho. Clark noted that the Clearwater was about 150 yards wide at that point, while the Snake (which he mistakenly thought was a continuation of the same Lewis's River where they had first met the Shoshone) was 250 yards wide at the point where the two rivers combined and flowed off toward the west. In his journal he noted a problem that would be a continuous source of irritation to him. "Our diet extremely bad having nothing but roots and dried fish to eate, all the Party have greatly the advantage of me, in as much as they all relish the flesh of the dogs."

*Clearwater River (left) entering the Snake River (c. 1890)*
*- Oregon Historical Society*

The numerous Indian villages they passed along the way were populated by Nez Percé and closely related tribes who increasingly showed great interest in the white strangers. From now on the expedition would be in the constant company of Indians. Twisted Hair and another Nez Percé chief named Tetoharsky preceded the party from village to village, assuring its residents of the white men's good intentions. Sacajawea continued to be invaluable. "The wife of Sharbono our interpetr we find reconciles all the Indians, as to our friendly intentions. A woman with a party of men is a token of peace."

For the next several days, they paddled down the Snake along the northern boundaries of what are now Asotin, Garfield, Columbia, and Walla Walla counties in Washington State, making almost thirty miles a day. They stopped only long enough to camp and to purchase fish and dogs at the various villages along the way. The problems they experienced in finding game were compounded by the fact that they were confined to the bottom of the river canyons. Countless sharp ridges and valleys ran down to the river on both sides except where they had broken off to form canyon walls faced with what Clark called "dark, rugged Stone." Clark worried about the wear and tear that would result from running the numerous rapids and wrote that they would have made more portages, "if the season was not so far advanced, and time so precious with us."

Wood for their campfires was a constant problem. The only trees they saw were the occasional small willows that grew along the riverbank. Then they emerged onto the virtually treeless Mid-Columbian shrub steppe, and the problem got worse. Both game and firewood were in short supply. Clark wrote, "The face of the Countrey on both Side of the river . . . contain but a Small preportion of herbage, no timber a few bushes excepted." One of the soldiers, John Ordway, wrote, "No timber. We can scarcely get wood enough to cook a little victuals."

On the thirteenth, they passed through a "long bad rapid in which the water is Confined in a Chanel of about 20 yards between the rugid rocks for the distance of a mile and a half." Once through those rapids they passed the mouth of the present-day Palouse River, which they named for their interpreter and hunter, George Drouillard. At the mouth of the river they found a large, abandoned Indian village. The house timbers had been carefully stored on scaffolds for reuse when their owners returned from the Blue Mountains, where they had gone to gather roots, pick berries, and hunt antelope. The stored timber was very valuable and had to be rafted down the river from where it had been cut in the foothills of the mountains. Like other local tribes, these Indians maintained a seasonal schedule of fishing, gathering, and hunting from early spring through late fall. In the winter, they lived in semi-subterranean, mat-covered lodges along the river.

On the morning of October 14 the party passed by a large rock shaped like the hull of a ship located near the present Lower Monumental Dam in Walla Walla County, Washington. Later that day, they lost a canoe when it struck a rock in a particularly bad stretch of rapids and dumped its occupants—including one of the Indian chiefs—into the river. Valuable supplies, including gunpowder, were lost, and what could be retrieved had to be laid out to dry. For the first time during the expedition, they were obliged to land and steal some wood from a vacant Indian structure in order to cook their meals. According to Clark, Twisted Hair and Tetoharsky gave them permission to use the wood. But at least Clark finally got a respite from the diet of dried fish and dog meat. He recorded in his journal that "for the first time for three weeks past I had a good dinner of Blue wing Teel."

The next day they continued to try to dry out their supplies. As the steep hills and canyons began to moderate, Lewis could now climb them to walk on the open plateau above the river, and he saw the Blue Mountains some sixty miles distant to the south. The expedition got underway again in the early afternoon, passing eleven islands and seven rapids, but making twenty miles before nightfall. Several days later, Clark climbed a high point and saw the snow-covered top of Mount Adams in the west for the first time.

The morning of October 16 dawned cool and cloudy. Rounded, grass-covered treeless hills replaced the canyon walls rising from the river on both sides. There were still more islands and rapids to be negotiated at the current location of Ice Harbor Dam, but then the river widened out. The party made about twenty-one miles before coming to a wide delta where the Snake emptied into the Columbia.

As they neared the junction of the two rivers, they were followed by growing numbers of curious Indians both in canoes and along the shore. The arrival of the strangers was causing a sensation among the Indians of the region. The area had long been a favorite place for the local tribes to fish, trade, and visit, but the arrival of the Corps of Discovery was something they had never seen before. A large village stood on the point of land that separated the Snake from the Columbia at what is now Sacajawea State Park, not far from the current-day city of Pasco, Washington. The explorers made camp nearby and welcomed a chief and 200 men and boys who came to see them, singing and dancing to the beat of their drums. The captains handed out tobacco to as many as possible and distributed Jefferson medals to the chiefs. To the west they saw the blue humps of the Horse Heaven Hills—formed during the Ice Age floods—about two miles distant on the other side of the Columbia River to the west.

# CHAPTER THREE

# Through the Mid-Columbia

THE EXCITEMENT SURROUNDING the expedition's arrival at the junction of the Snake and Columbia Rivers seemed not to be shared by the explorers themselves. Lewis had stopped writing in his journal after his emergence from the Bitterroots. Clark, in his matter-of-fact manner, simply recorded, "S. 28 W. 6 ½ miles to the Junction of Columbia R." It is true that the confluence had been correctly predicted by the Indians traveling with them, but a little more enthusiasm could have been expected in recording such a milestone. Private Whitehouse wrote, "Toward evening we arrived at a large fork that came into this River from a Northerly direction & was much large[r] than the fork which we descended which we supposed to be the Columbia River."

The captains had cause to be concerned. They believed that they had already been *on* the Columbia River—that the Snake was the Columbia. Could this larger river coming in from the north be the same river that Alexander Mackenzie had discovered twelve years earlier? If so, did that validate the existing British claim to the region and render irrelevant one of the vital goals of their expedition? They had a copy of Mackenzie's 1801 *Voyages* report with them, and they consulted it carefully, but there was little they could do about it at the time. Winter was closing in, and they needed to reach the ocean.

The Indians they encountered at the junction included large numbers of Walla Wallas, Yakamas, and Wanapums, drawn to the river by the fall salmon migration. Clark noted, in various journal entries, the differences between these Indians and those they had previously met during their travels. These Indians were smaller in stature. They wore fewer clothes and owned more canoes than horses. They lived in triangular-shaped lodges of various lengths, about six feet tall, with relatively flat roofs and interior wooden frames covered with tule reed mats. Clark noted, "The roughfs [roofs] are nearly flat, which proves to me that rains are not common in this open Countrey."

Clark observed one blind woman who was said to be more than 100 years old. He also noticed that the tribe's teeth were worn to the gum line by the time the Indians reached middle age. This has been attributed to the fact that the frequent local winds carried fine sands that were deposited on the dying salmon (and everything else) and acted as an abrasive on the teeth when the fish were eaten.

The local Indians owned large numbers of dogs, which, in the absence of available game, the explorers purchased to supplement their diet of dried or fresh salmon. Clark had problems with either option. Fresh fish would have been preferable to the dried and pounded salmon, but "The fish being out of season and dying in great numbers in the rivers, we did not think it proper to use them." Nor was he a fan of dog meat. "As for my own part, I have not become reconciled to the taste of this animal."

The next day, October 17, Clark decided to explore the river on a clear and pleasant day. Having heard from the Indians about another river that flowed into the Columbia farther to the north, he set out with two men in the small canoe and paddled north for about ten miles. They passed numerous islands, most of which are no longer visible because of the higher water levels created by the pool behind McNary Dam. They stopped at one island located off the north bank of the river, which had three mat lodges and many women occupied with "great quants. of Salmon on Scaffolds drying." The Indians prepared a lunch of salmon boiled in a basket, with hot rocks from the fire. Clark declared that "The boiled fish . . . was delicious."

Clark explored the mouth of what is now the Yakima River where it enters the Columbia at present-day Richland, Washington. He wrote, "This river is remarkably clear and crowded with salmon in many places . . . Salmon may be seen to the depth of 15 or 20 feet . . .

The number . . . is incredible to say." He returned to camp at dusk and "shot a Fowl of the Pheasent kind as large as a (Small) turkey." It was most likely a sage grouse.

In his journal entry for October 17, Clark continued his descriptions of the local Indians. The "women are more inclined to Copulency than any we have yet Seen, with low Stature broad faces, heads flattened (the eyes back) and the forward compressed so as to form a Streight line from the nose to the Crown of the head."

Before they left the confluence, they measured the width of the two rivers. They found the Columbia to be about a half mile (960 yards) wide at that point, while the Snake was determined to be 575 yards wide. For comparison purposes, today the Columbia River is about one mile wide at this location.

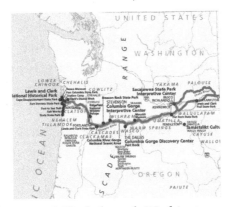

*Route of Lewis and Clark through Washington and Oregon.*
*Credit: National Park Service*

On the eighteenth, they began to stock up on provisions for their trip down the Columbia. "The fish being out of Season, we purchased forty dogs for which we gave articles of little value," Clark wrote. Underway at last, they paddled past more islands and more fishing camps and winter villages, past the mouth of the Walla Walla River, which joined the Columbia from the east.

Here the land on both sides of the river began to rise to heights of 200 feet or more with dark outcroppings of basalt rock. From a vantage point on the high land above the river, Clark saw what must have been Mount Hood ("a mountain bearing S.W. Conocal form Covered with Snow"). The mountain had been named after a British admiral by Royal Navy Lieutenant William Broughton, who entered and explored the lower portions of the Columbia in 1792. Finally, the Corps of Discovery had entered the blank gap on the map that separated lands they had already explored and the easternmost point on the river mapped by Broughton in 1792.

They continued on past frequent clusters of Indian lodges, fishing platforms, and racks for drying salmon. The members of the expedition continued to be surprised by the number of Indians they encountered. On the night of the eighteenth, they camped and were soon informed by Twisted Hair that Yelleppit, the principal chief of the Wallula (Walla Walla) Indians, wanted to meet them.

He arrived with two sub-chiefs and twenty Indians early the next morning. Clark described him as a "bold handsom Indian, with a dignified countenance about 35 years of age, about 5 feet 8 inches high and well perpotioned." His hospitality appeared to be every bit as friendly as that of the Yakamas and Wanapums before him. Private Cruzatte's violin and Clark's slave, York, continued to amaze and entertain their guests. Yelleppit wanted them to stay longer, but the captains, wanting to press on, promised to spend more time with them on their return trip and set out early the next morning.

They were now in the Wallula Gap, the narrow passageway where the Columbia cuts through the Horse Heaven Hills. On either side of the river, the tall canyon walls rose more than fifteen hundred feet and obscured the barren plateau of bunch grass and sagebrush above—the Mid-Columbia shrub steppe. Hills and broken terrain characterized the Oregon side, while more basalt walls obstructed views of the Washington side of the river. The land flattened out as the river finally turned to the west, past Hat Rock—a rock formation shaped like an Indian hat—on the left before reaching a two-mile long set of rapids (Umatilla Rapids) at the present-day site of McNary Dam and the city of Umatilla on the Oregon side.

After completing their portage around the rapids, Clark shot a Sandhill crane and noticed large numbers of Indians in a village on the

Washington side of the river. He took three men in their smallest dugout canoe to paddle to the village of Umatillas located near what is now the town of Plymouth, Washington. He entered the largest of the mat lodges and found more than thirty Indians huddled inside, riveted by fear.

Maybe it was hearing the sound of a gun for the first time, or seeing the crane fall from the sky, or Clark's use of glass to light his peace pipe, but they were in dire fear for their lives. It took Lewis arriving with Sacajawea to calm them. Once again, having a woman in the party "confirmed those people of our friendly intentions, as no woman ever accompanies a war party of Indians in the quarter," Clark wrote.

Two days later, on October 20, they reached what is now Crow Butte Park, located in western Benton County, Washington. Increasingly, the Washington side of the river presented "high rugged hills," Clark noted, while on the Oregon side there was "a low plain and not a tree to be seen in any direction." There were more ducks available for dinner than there was fuel available to cook them. Now they were making good time—forty-two miles on the nineteenth, and thirty-six on the twentieth.

*Hat Rock.*
*Credit: Oregon Historical Society*

On the twenty-first, they met Indians who sold them some welcome driftwood but also warned them of a great falls ahead. Clark noted that "All [the natives] have *pierced noses* and the men when Dressed ware a long taper'd piece of Shell [dentalium] or beed put through the nose."

They passed through more rapids crowded with large rocks and camped on the Washington side below the mouth of the small John Day River and the current site of John Day Dam, which was completed in 1971. That night in camp beneath the high hills and "scattered trees," they enjoyed an unusual treat—some homemade beer made from bread, which had gotten wet and fermented, that the Nez Percé had given one of the privates.

On October 22, they passed through a series of rapids and islands and saw even more Indian lodges—some up to sixty feet long and supported by interior wooden frames. For the first time, some of the Indians wore articles of western apparel, such as sailor jackets, hats, and brass bracelets. The expedition passed the spot where the US 97 highway bridge now connects Biggs Junction on the Oregon side with the small community of Maryhill, with its orchards and vineyards, on the Washington side.

Perched high on the hillside is Maryhill mansion, built in 1914 as the home of the railroad tycoon James J. Hill, president of the Great Northern Railway. Now an eclectic art museum, it includes a reproduction of Stonehenge, honoring the dead soldiers of the First World War.

Always attuned for new words, the explorers now kept encountering another one, "timm." It meant big falls in the river. And big they were! They found the first of them six miles beyond the Deschutes River, which entered from the Oregon side, when they finally came face to face with Celilo Falls, the "Great Falls of the Columbia," located in a narrow channel between the small town of Wishram on the Washington side and the Celilo Village of Wasco Indians on the Oregon side. Clark provided a vivid description of the falls in his journal entry of October 22:

We landed and walked down accompanied by an old man to view the falls, and the best rout for to make a portage . . . the waters is divided into Several narrow channels which pass through a hard black rock forming Islands of rocks at this State of the water, on these Islands of rocks as well as at and about their Lodges I observe great numbers of Stacks of pounded Salmon neatly preserved.

*B. A. Gifford, Indians fishing at Celilo Falls (c. 1905).*
*Credit: Oregon Historical Society*

The captains spent most of October 23 completing the 1,200-foot-long portage around the falls. They decided to make the trip on the Washington side, and Indians from below provided horses and people to help with the heavy packages. The canoes were carried around on the Oregon side, and in places they used elk-skin ropes to lower the canoes while hundreds of Indians looked on in anticipation of an accident from which they might materially benefit. On both sides of the river, the men were tortured by millions of fleas, which were so bad that the men had to strip off their clothes in order to try—mostly unsuccessfully—to escape them.

# CHAPTER FOUR

# Crossroads of the Columbia

BELOW THE FALLS the river widened into a large basin dominated by a "tremendous black rock" (Brown's Island) where the river narrowed into a channel Clark estimated at "not exceeding forty five yards wide." Later travelers have estimated that it might have been twice that wide. This was the Ten Mile Rapids or Short Narrows—two and one-half miles below Celilo Falls. Invisible now under the pool behind The Dalles Dam, this was the first in a series of violent cascades and rapids known collectively as The Narrows or The Dalles, which stretched for nearly twelve miles. The height of the river fell between sixty and eighty feet depending on the season.

Before attempting the rapids, the expedition camped on the Washington side at what is now Horsethief Lake State Park, east of the current town of Dallesport, and planned for the inevitable. Clark continued in his journal: "I determined to pass through this place notwithstanding the horrid appearance of the agitated gut swelling, boiling & whorling in every direction." Clark sent the men who could not swim ashore with the supplies they could not afford to lose to make the portage around the rapids on land while he proceeded to run the rapids two canoes at a time. "We passed Safe to the astonishment of all the Inds."

Once below the falls the captains made their first contact with the Chinook-speaking Wishram and Wasco Indians, whose canoes—lightweight, but able to carry heavy loads because of their unique construction—were "neeter made than any I have ever Seen and

Calculated to ride the waves, and carry emence burthens." Lewis immediately traded their smallest pine log dugout canoe, plus a hatchet and some trade goods, to get his hands on one.

In camp that night, the Nez Percé chiefs, Twisted Hair and Tetoharsky, reported hearing rumors that the Indians who lived below the falls (Upper Chinooks) intended to attack them. They correctly said that this location represented the boundary between their world and the one occupied by "the nations below." They asked to go home. The captains, concerned, made sure that all of the party's muskets were in order and issued extra ammunition. Their fears might have been aggravated by the trade tensions between the tribes, but the chiefs also knew that this boundary between the two Indian peoples marked the end of their linguistic ability to serve as interpreters.

On the twenty-fourth, the expedition came upon a village of approximately twenty wooden lodges on the north bank of the river. The lodges were scattered around a long, obviously artificial thirty-foot high mound, called Wakemap by the Indians. This was the location of the ancient village of Wishram (not to be confused with the current town of the same name located upriver across from the Deschutes River). The Indians called it Nixluidix, meaning trading place.

The village was strategically located at the boundary between the Sahaptian-speaking Indians of the upper river and the Chinookian-speaking Indians of the lower river and the coast. Giant rocks above the cataracts provided ledges for wooden fishing platforms where huge numbers of salmon could be gaffed or netted, but even more important, the area served as a melting pot for the cultures that fished and traded there.

Concerned by the warnings of the Nez Percé chiefs the night before, Clark decided to visit the village but was warmly received. He was invited to enter one of the plank houses. The structures were about thirty feet long and sunk six feet into the ground, their wooden plank roofs supported by long poles resting on sturdy upright log supports at the corners and on each end of the structure. More split wooden planks formed the walls. Light entered through an opening in the roof, which also allowed the smoke from the internal fire pit to escape. Each house appeared to be occupied by about three families. The party's most capable carpenter, Patrick Gass, wrote that Wishram was filled with "tolerably comfortable houses." They were the first wooden houses the explorers had seen since they left Illinois.

Clark called the place a "great mart of trade" and estimated that he saw 10,000 pounds of fish drying on wooden racks above the river. What corn and buffalo were to the Missouri villages, dried salmon was to Wishram and Wasco merchants who lived between Celilo Falls and The Dalles. They were the middle men in a vast trading network that stretched from the Pacific coast to the Nez Percé—and through them to the Shoshone and the tribes of the middle Missouri—in an intricate web of personal and economic relationships.

Dried fish, wapato bread, camas root, and European trade goods flowed east, while horses, buffalo meat and robes, hide clothing, and bear grass for cooking baskets and making the distinct wide-brimmed northwest coast hats flowed west. Alexander Ross, one of John Jacob Astor's fur traders who visited the rendezvous a decade later, estimated that 3,000 Indians were present at peak trading periods.

Lewis and Clark arrived too late in the season to experience the full flavor of the Indian rendezvous at The Dalles, but the smell of fish and the great hordes of fleas remained as testimony of what had transpired. Each year the tribes came—from the east rode the Cayuse, the Nez Percé and, occasionally, visitors from even farther away. From the west came the coastal tribes in their graceful canoes—all to meet in a month-long conclave to fish, trade, fornicate, and gamble among the rocks on the river.

Safely through the Short Narrows, Lewis and Clark now had to tackle the "Grand Dalles," or Long Narrows of the Columbia, where the river narrowed from a half mile wide to about 240 feet. Emery and Ruth Strong write in their *Seeking Western Waters* that the explorers saw the savage whirlpool that resulted from the narrowing river engulf an entire house. It disappeared, only to be spit out a half mile below as a few splintered boards.

The captains surveyed the situation and determined that a portage with their large canoes was impractical. They would unload their most valuable articles and run the canoes through. Clark explained how they divided their party:

> Some to take over the Canoes, and others to take our Stores across the portage of a mile to a place below this bad whorl & Suck, with Some others I had vexed on the Chanel with roapes to throw out to any who Should unfortunately meet with difficuely in passing through.

The first three canoes made it without difficulty. The fourth nearly filled with water. The final canoe passed through by taking on some water. Clark wrote with understatement, "thus Safely below what I conceved to be the worst part of this chanel felt my self extreamly gratified and pleased."

*The Long Narrows.*
*Credit: Oregon Historical Society*

Later that day they arrived at the present location of The Dalles, Oregon, and set up camp on a rock island near the mouth of Mill Creek, north of what is now the Lewis and Clark Festival Park. They stayed there between October 25 and October 27 while they dried their cargo and patched their canoes. They called the camp "Fort Rock."

The next night they were visited by a delegation of Indians, led by a man the captains described as "the principal chief from the nation below." The chief was young and handsome, and many of his companions wore pieces of western clothing. After sharing a pipe and presenting medals, the captains believed that they had successfully negotiated a peace between the Nez Percé and the Chinooks, followed by dancing to Pierre Cruzatte's fiddle. At that point, the group finally bid farewell to Twisted Hair and Tetoharsky, who were anxious to leave, and vowed to see them again on their return. The chiefs bought some local horses and rode upriver toward home.

Lewis and Clark failed to understand the complex nature of the tribal relationships among the Indians. Like the Teton Sioux on the upper Missouri, the Chinooks sought to control the flow of trade along the river. Lewis and Clark had immediately understood the potential threat they faced from the Sioux and dealt with it, but they were much less aware of the complex situation that now faced them.

The Chinooks had long traded with American and European ship captains who called at the mouth of the Columbia, and were no longer in awe of whites. As a matter of fact they would have considered white men coming from the east a significant threat because they represented a potential rival source of manufactured goods that would be available to the inland tribes without having to trade with the Chinooks.

For their part, Lewis and Clark held these river Indians in low esteem, with the exception of their obvious dexterity as canoeists. Petty theft had been a problem for the expedition since they had entered the Columbia, but it became a much more serious matter as the party traveled between Celilo Falls and the Cascade River Gorge.

During the frequent portages, anything that was laid aside for the moment was quickly gone. Sergeant Ordway wrote, "The natives are very troublesome about our camp." When confronted, they became sullen and resentful because they believed that the intruders could well afford the loss of a blanket, a hatchet, or even a gun because they had so many of them. It was their way of charging a toll for the right of passage, while lacking the military power to openly enforce it.

The captains responded by severely limiting the number of Indians allowed to visit their camp at any one time and posting armed guards at night. Their precautions did not go unnoticed. As the Americans struggled through the Short and Long Narrows, the Indians approached them with much more caution.

On the twenty-seventh, they set out again downriver, entering the foothills of the Cascade Range, with pine trees increasingly plentiful on the brown hills. With ample fuel they began to find some relief from their diet of fish and dogs. Deer and other small animals, along with the ever-present salmon, were now plentiful. For the first time, they encountered snow geese and swans, oceangoing steelhead trout, and mountain goats. The constant noise produced by the migratory waterfowl was deafening. "I could not sleep for the noise kept [up] by the swans [and] ducks. They were immensely numerous and their cries horrid," Clark complained one morning.

They knew that they were getting close to the Pacific. They now had stunning views of Mount Hood, which they had only seen at a distance from the eastern plateaus. They were entering an area of the river that had earlier been viewed from far away and drawn on British maps. The Great Falls and rapids had been correctly forecast by the Indians. By their calculations, they had fewer than 200 miles to go before they reached the Pacific.

CHAPTER FIVE

# Into the Gorge and on to the Sea

ON THEY PRESSED, through more rapids and rock-lined cataracts, into the Columbia River Gorge as it squeezed its way through the Cascade Mountains. The Corps of Discovery made only four miles the day after leaving Fort Rock, due to high winds and the realization that the design of their bulky dugout canoes was going to be a continuing problem on the river. On October 29, they came upon four miles of rapids filled with chutes and falls that Clark described as "water passing with great velocity forming and boiling in a most horrible manner." They crossed the point where the Klickitat River flows into the Columbia at the present-day town of Lyle on the Washington side. Then they passed the Hood River on the Oregon side, where it enters the Columbia at the town of the same name.

Now they had entered an extremely different world. Gone were the basalt rock outcroppings and empty prairies of the Mid-Columbia shrub steppe; gone were the grassy hills and scattered ponderosa pines around The Dalles. Now the tall hills were topped by snow and covered in fir, spruce, and alder, with a solid mass of evergreen shrubs in various hues of green. There was more game, and huge numbers of migratory waterfowl flew overhead and rested in the quiet coves along the banks of the river. It was November and the days were often foggy, clearing only in the afternoon. When it wasn't foggy, it was often because a storm front blew through with gray skies and sheets of rain.

They were visited continuously by the local Indians, who continued to make a poor impression on the members of the expedition, particularly when they were compared with the friendly Mandans and handsome Indians from the upper Missouri. These Indians, though generally friendly, tended toward sullenness and thievery. Now without interpreters, the expedition was at the mercy of the Indians and dependent on them to sell them food. They had to rely on their ability to communicate their friendly intentions through sign language, the distribution of gifts, and a ceremonial smoke from Clark's treasured pipe.

On October 30, they were able to proceed fifteen miles down the river but camped wet and uncomfortable on an island located between the present towns of Stevenson and Cascade Locks. The river narrowed here as they passed through the Cascades. Clark recorded that they were obliged to portage "940 yards of bad Slippery and rocky way" and then had to muscle their canoes over logs and rocks around what they called the "great shute."

This channel is wider today because of the water in Lake Bonneville and is spanned by the Bridge of the Gods, built in 1920. The channel opens to a jumble of rock islands on which the Bonneville Dam—the first of the great hydroelectric dams on the Columbia—was built in 1937. Here, steep, tree-covered mountains rose from the banks of the river on the Oregon side and were only slightly less dramatic on the Washington side as they climbed to the snow-covered cap of Mount St. Helens.

*The "Great Shute" of the Cascades.*
*Credit: Oregon Historical Society*

The next day dawned wet and cloudy again. They reached Beacon Rock, also known as Castle Rock—the core of an extinct volcano rising 848 feet from the Columbia River—which had first been sighted by Lieutenant William Boughton in 1792. A little farther on they would have seen the dramatic Multnomah Falls on the Oregon side, dropping 620 feet to the river below before camping for the night at what is now Rooster Rock State Park. By now, they were through the worst of the gorge, and the river began to widen as it backed up from the sea. For the first time since they had wintered with the Mandans, they were passing through country that had been previously mapped by whites.

*Beacon Rock.*
*Credit: Oregon Historical Society*

On November 1, they stopped to repair their canoes and dry their gear. And now they encountered yet another first—large numbers of sea otters feasting on the salmon run. Clark took the time to write extensively about the local Indians. "I can't lern whether these Indians trade with white people or Inds. Below for the Beeds & copper, which they are so fond of." He noted that they were short, suffered from bad teeth and blindness, and had high cheeks, pierced noses, and flattened heads. "The women [are] Small and homely, many of them [with] Sweled legs, large about the knees,—owing to the position in which they Set upon their hams." They lived in large plank houses, thirty to fifty feet square, with an arched entry, about thirty inches high. The interiors were decorated with images cut of wood, often of humans.

The next day they made almost ten miles and camped at the mouth of the Sandy River across the river from where the Washougal empties into the Columbia from the north. They made much better progress the next day, reaching the mouth of the Willamette River, but not realizing it because an island blocked it from view. The land here was low, particularly on the Oregon side, and cut through with sloughs and marshes created by the Willamette delta.

On the night of November 4, the expedition encountered a large group of Skilloot Indians, another Chinook-speaking tribe that lived between the Washougal and Cowlitz Rivers. Some wore blue and red blankets, while others wore sailor's jackets and hats. One man even wore his hair in a short queue like a sailor. They were armed with war axes, spears, bows, and arrows. Some had muskets and pistols. Clark sensed the potential for a confrontation and wrote, "Those fellows we found assumeing and disagreeable." However, "we smoked with them and treated them with every attention & friendship."

The situation changed for the worse when Clark discovered that one of the visitors had "Stold my pipe Tomahawk which They were Smoking with." Another made off with a hooded wool blanket coat belonging to one of the men. A search produced the coat, but not Clark's treasured ceremonial pipe tomahawk. The expedition kept to the river until an hour after dark "with a view to get clear of the natives who [were] constantly around us, and troublesome."

This experience colored their relations with the local Indians throughout the winter and during their return upriver in the spring of 1806. The impression had been building since they entered the Columbia that these river Indians were incorrigible thieves. To make matters worse, they completely misunderstood the motivations of the Chinooks, who felt that the whites could easily cope with what they lost and that what they took was a form of payment for passage down the river.

The Chinooks also had the benefit of knowing that the whites depended on the Indians to sell them food, but the explorers resented paying what they considered to be "immoderate prices" for it. Another reason for mistrust and suspicion was that the men of the expedition viewed the local Indians through the filter of their Euro-American values. There was much about the Indians of the northern plains that they had found praiseworthy, but the customs and practices of these Indians were considered incomprehensible and reprehensible.

The expedition traveled about thirty miles a day as they proceeded down the river past countless native villages. Wary from their recent unpleasant encounter with the Skilloots and anxious to get down the river, they limited their visits to these villages to trading for food. Increasingly, they were amazed by the degree to which contact with whites had influenced the Indian people. They owned many American- and European-made objects. They repeated profane words and phrases they could only have learned from seaman. One even had the name "J. Bowmon" tattooed on his arm.

On November 5, they encountered their first coastal canoes—much larger than any they had seen on the river. The largest had a bear's image carved on its decorative bow. On November 7, they set off in the morning fog. By afternoon, the skies had cleared and Clark saw what he believed was the ocean for the first time. "Ocian in view! O! the joy," he famously wrote in his journal. It was a false alarm. What he actually saw was a portion of the Columbia River estuary where the river widened to almost twelve miles across and was affected by the tides and long rollers that came in directly from the ocean.

Sacajawea was seasick from the motion of the waves on the cumbersome pine log canoes. The water was too salty to drink. No matter—they had plenty of rainwater. In his journal, Clark recorded his reckoning of the miles they had traveled since May 1804: "Ocian 4142 Miles from the Mouth of Missouri R."

The next day they were crossing the wide mouth of Gray's Bay on the north side of the Columbia River estuary when a driving windstorm whipped up waves too large for them to navigate in their pine log canoes. They made an emergency landing and camped just east of Point Ellice on a narrow ledge of land among huge logs that were "nearly 200 feet long and 4 to 7 feet thick."

Pebbles and small rocks, loosened by the wind and rain, fell on them from the cliff above. They erected such shelter as was possible but had to endure ten days on the open beach in the face of gale-force winds and driving rain. The storm didn't keep the Indians away, however. They came to trade salmon for fishhooks. Clark referred to site as "this dismal nitch" and wrote that it was "the most disagreeable time I have experienced confined on a tempiest coast wet, where I can neither get out to hunt, return to a better situation, or proceed on."

*"This dismal nitch" campsite to the east of Point Ellis.*
*Credit: National Park Service*

The sun arrived with the morning of the fifteenth, and they were finally able to get their small Indian canoe—which rode the waves better—out and around the headland of Gray's Bay to hunt for a better campsite. They located a sandy beach with a small stream and abandoned, flea-infested Indian dwellings where a safe camp, if not a dry one, could be established. Sources conflict as to the location of this camp. Some say it was located just below Chinook Point on the east side of Baker's Bay, while others place it near McKenzie Head on Cape Disappointment. In any event, they could now see, when the weather allowed, the full panorama of the mouth of the Columbia River between Point Adams and Cape Disappointment. Lewis could contain himself no longer. He took a party to search for the elusive trading post or a ship at the river's mouth.

Actually, they had just missed one. Weeks after they moved across the river to camp for the winter at Fort Clatsop, the *Lydia* out of Boston came over the bar and passed some of their former campsites without knowing it. The Indians told the sailors of their recent visitors and showed them a Jefferson medal they had received, but didn't tell them that Lewis and Clark were still in the area. The ship went on to trade at Nootka Bay. When it returned in the spring, the Indians gave the captain one of the summaries of the expedition and formal notifications that the captains had prepared and left with the Indians for just this purpose. But it was too late to make contact. Lewis and Clark had already left for home. Determining that no ship or trading post was at the mouth of the Columbia, the explorers named the peninsula Cape Disappointment.

One day, several Clatsop Indian chiefs visited their camp. One of them wore a magnificent sea-otter coat that Clark declared was "more butiful than any fur I had ever Seen." Both captains bid for the coat. The chief refused their offers, pointing to Sacajawea's belt of blue beads. It is unclear who ended up with the sea-otter coat, but Sacajawea received a new coat made of blue cloth in return for her beads. Believing that the whites would pay almost anything for the coats, the Indians returned with more, but the price was beyond what the captains could afford. Clark recorded that he was amazed when one turned down a watch, a handkerchief, a bunch of red beads, and a dollar in American coin.

Their hopes of finding a trading post or a ship dashed, they had to make a decision about a winter camp. They couldn't survive if they had to buy their food from local Indians at inflated prices throughout the winter. They would have to wait until the mountain snows melted in the spring, so they were in no hurry to begin their return trip.

They wanted to find a camp with fresh water and adequate game. The Indians had indicated that elk were more plentiful on the Oregon side, whereas deer were more plentiful on the Washington side. The decision was easy: Elk were bigger and easier to hunt, and their skins were better for clothing. There was another factor too. The captains wanted to be close enough to the ocean to contact a trading ship if one appeared.

They put it to a vote. Everyone, including York and Sacajawea, cast a vote. One of the men voted to stay on the Washington side. Others wanted to return upriver for the winter. The majority was convinced by the captain's reasoning to move over to the Oregon side. Sacajawea voted to winter at a place that had plenty of roots for cooking.

They broke camp on November 25 and retraced their steps for two days, past Pillar Rock until they reached the site of their earlier encampment on November 7.They crossed over to the Oregon side and traveled down the river, camping near the present city of Astoria, Oregon, but without finding a satisfactory location on the shores of Young's Bay or up Young's River.

Lewis finally found a suitable campsite on a small bluff with a spring and good timber located about 200 feet back from the west bank of what is now the Lewis and Clark River, about three miles from where it entered the Columbia. It would become Fort Clatsop. Lewis marked the occasion by carving his name on a tree. The other men did likewise. Clark improved Lewis's inscription by adding: "William Clark December 3rd 1805. By land from the U. States in 1804 & 1805."

CHAPTER SIX

# Winter Camp

ALL OF THE accounts—those written then and since—agree on one thing: the time the Corps of Discovery spent at Fort Clatsop during the winter of 1805–1806 was miserable. Gone was the sense of anticipation and excitement that been present at Fort Mandan a year earlier. Maybe it was because the time they spent at Fort Clatsop was anticlimactic after reaching the Pacific—something to be endured until they could head for home. The weather certainly didn't help. Between December 8, 1805, and March 23, 1806, it rained all but twelve days. Only six days were partly sunny.

On the morning of the December 8, 1805, after camping at the site Lewis had selected, the captains separated. Clark, hearing the "roar" of the ocean from camp, left for the coast with a few men to find a suitable place to make salt. Lewis and the rest of the party remained to cut down the trees needed to build the huts and palisades of what would become Fort Clatsop. It was not until December 14 that they had enough to begin splitting logs. Fortunately, the characteristics of the trees made that part of the work easy. Patrick Gass wrote that the wood made "the finest puncheons (split wood boards) I have ever seen."

Other aspects of their situation were more difficult. Their clothes and bedding were mildewed and rotted. Some of the men were sick or injured. The fleas that had accompanied them from various Indian villages made sleep difficult. The weather was terrible! On December 16, Clark wrote in his journal after a particularly miserable day.

> I had the two canoes loaded with 11 Elk which was brought to the canoes . . . the winds violent. Trees falling in every direction, whorl winds, with gusts of rain, Hail & Thunder, this kind of weather lasted all day. Certainly one of the worst days that ever was!

Their relations with their new neighbors were problematic. Within days, groups of Indians began visiting the new camp. Coboway, the chief of a nearby Clatsop village, visited on the twelfth, wanting to trade. His prices were reasonable one day and grossly overpriced the next. At least he was friendly enough and got along well with Clark.

On December 24, another young Clatsop leader named Cuscalah came with his brother and two women. They wanted to sell roots, but the captains felt that their asking price was too high. Then Cuscalah tried to sell the services of the two women, "which we also declined axcpting which also displeased them . . . the female part appeared to be highly disgusted at our refuseing of their favours &tc." They were also visited by a young, freckle-faced man, about twenty-five years old, with red hair, whom Clark described as "half white at least." This individual later became well known to the Astoria fur traders, who arrived six years after Lewis and Clark left, as Jack Ramsay. He was not hard to identify. His name was tattooed on his arm. It was thought that he was the issue of shipwrecked Americans or Europeans who were taken in by the Clatsops.

They began moving into the still-unfinished fort on December 23. Completed, it measured about fifty feet square with two long, facing structures on either side joined by a log palisade on either end. A main gate was located in the palisade that connected the two structures on one of the squares, while a smaller entrance was cut into the other in order to gain access to the nearby spring. An interior parade ground separated the two structures. One of the huts was separated into three spaces for the enlisted men, while the other was divided into four spaces: one for the captains; another for Charbonneau, Sacajawea, and her son; a third for the orderly room, and the fourth for the smokehouse.

On Christmas morning, 1805, the men woke their leaders with a celebratory volley, a shout, and a song. They exchanged some simple presents, but there was not much else to sustain their holiday mood. Clark explained, "We would have spent this day in . . . feasting, had we any thing either to raise our Sperits or even gratify our appetites, our dinner concisted of pore Elk. So much Spoiled that we eate it thro' mear necessity."

Three days later they dispatched a small party of salt makers to a site Clark had selected in what is now Seaside, Oregon. The process entailed boiling seawater in kettles until it evaporated, then scraping the salt from the sides of the pots and collecting it in waterproof packages made from hides. Laboriously, they produced twenty gallons of salt before the site was abandoned on February 21.

On December 29, the monotony was broken by word that a whale had washed up on the beach near Tillamook Head. Lewis immediately determined to go to the site in the hope of recovering oil and blubber, but the winds were so high for the next week that he was forced to remain in camp. The fort was finally completed on December 30.

With the exception of three short entries in late December, it had been sixty-seven days since Lewis had written a word about the expedition. His silence has been a subject of conjecture for historians and biographers ever since. Some have speculated that he kept journals during that time but that they were subsequently lost. Clark didn't comment on the lapse.

*Haystack Rock off Cannon Beach, Oregon.*
*It was near here that the whale washed up on the beach.*
*Credit: Wikipedia Commons*

Most historians now believe that Lewis just quit writing. With the exception of his illness resulting from his change of diet while with the Shoshones and the Nez Percé, he had not been physically incapacitated. Lewis remained an active leader, fully exercising his authority. Many argue that he was a manic-depressive, a disorder than ran in his family and might have contributed to his violent death just three years later. For whatever reason, Lewis couldn't summon the energy to write during this period.

It is certainly fascinating that the man who made sure that he was the first to describe in vivid detail the Great Falls of the Missouri, the Gates of the Mountains, the Three Forks, and the Shoshone didn't take pains to describe the Nez Percé, the Mid-Columbia shrub steppe, the Great Falls of the Columbia, or even the first view of the Pacific Ocean.

But on the first day of the new year—the year in which Lewis expected to return home—he finally resumed writing in his journal.

Indeed, his words now flowed, like a pent-up river, from the tip of his quill pen. He began with a detailed description of the Steller's jay and then moved on to a passage that suggested a hint of homesickness:

> Our repast of this day, tho' better than that of Christmass, consisted principally in the anticipation of the 1st day of January 1807, when in the bosom of our friends we hope to participate in the mirth and hilarity of the day, and when with the zest given by the recollection of the present, we shall completely, both mentally and corporally, enjoy the repast which the hand of civilization has prepared for us.

The beginning of the new year was as if a heavy blanket had been lifted from him. This would be the year they would return home. From that point on, his thoughts and actions were focused on that goal.

But first, he had to deal with the unavoidable delay created by their need to winter at Fort Clatsop. He penned a series of special orders governing the operation of the fort and relationships with local Indians. The gate would be closed and locked at sunset. No Indians would be permitted to remain in the fort overnight without the captains' express permission. An armed guard would be posted each night to ensure the fort's security. Clark noted that the Indians received this news with "reluctance."

The men were ordered to "treat the natives in a friendly manner," but the arrival and activities of all Indians were to be carefully monitored. The sergeant of the guard was authorized "to imploy such coercive measures (not extending to the taking of life) as shall in his discretion be deemed necessary."

Despite the new rules, the local Clatsops, and sometimes visiting Chinooks, still paid social visits to the fort, but the relationships were much less convivial than those the party had enjoyed with the Mandans a year earlier. The men had frequent sexual contact with the local women, but Lewis was concerned that familiarity would, over time, trump vigilance, and he continued to remind them to keep their guard up.

Neither Lewis nor Clark spent much time visiting the nearby Indian villages. The central reason again appears to have been their attitudes about their Indian neighbors. The captains distrusted and generally disliked most of them. This seems to have been best articulated in another passage. Lewis wrote, "Notwithstanding their apparent friendly disposition, their great averice and hope of plunder might induce them to be treacherous. At all events we determined always to be on our guard . . . and never place ourselves at the mercy of any savages."

Keenly judging the needs of their new neighbors, the Indians started bringing food, stacks of woven, wide-brimmed hats, bags, mats, and the occasional dog instead of the more expensive fur pelts to trade. But even these trading trips were infrequent. During the three-and-a-half months Lewis and Clark spent at Fort Clatsop, the Indians came specifically to trade only twenty-four times.

One of the few memorable events to take place that winter occurred on the night of January 8. Private McNeal decided to go to a nearby Indian lodge for some whale blubber and "something better." But when a woman tried to hold him down inside a blanket, he fought to get free, and she screamed, alarming the garrison. Lewis recorded that Clark sent "Sergt. Pryor & 4 men in quest of Mc.Neal, who' they met comeing across the Creek in great hast." All assumed that McNeal was being murdered for his meager possessions, but it was soon understood that he had just been acting stupidly. Clark named the creek "McNeal's folley."

By January 10, the weather had abated enough for Clark to set out with a party of eleven men to find the carcass of the whale that had washed up on the ocean beach. Sacajawea demanded that she be allowed to go along.

> The Indian woman was very importunate to be permitted to go, and was therefore indulged; she observed that she had traveled a long way with us to

see the great waters, and that now that the monstrous fish was also to be seen, she thought it very hard she could not be permitted to see either.

By the time they got to the whale, it had been thoroughly picked over by the local Indians, but Clark was able (with difficulty and a small bag of trade goods he brought along) to buy 300 pounds of blubber and a little oil, which he brought back to the fort.

Soon both the blubber and the oil were gone, and the party was back to the daily monotony of its prison-like fort. Lewis made no recorded excursions from the fort, and his journal entities are full of the boredom he must have felt. The captains habitually wrote that "nothing worthy of notice occurred today." On January 18: "No . . . occurrence worthy of relation took place [today]. On February 2: "Not any occurrence today worthy of notice."

On March 3: "No movement of the party today worthy of notice. Every thing moves on in the old way and we are counting the days which seperate us from the first of April (their scheduled departure date) and what bind us to Fort Clatsop."

Their diet contributed to their boredom. During the three-and-a-half months they lived at Fort Clatsop, they killed 131 elk, twenty deer, a few beaver, an otter, and a raccoon. Occasionally they purchased a few dogs. It is surprising that they ate little or no fish. Because of the weather the meat spoiled quickly, so Lewis ordered that it be jerked so that it would last longer.

If Lewis and Clark were what James Ronda called "reluctant traders and inactive diplomats," they had plenty of time to write and work on their maps. Stephen Ambrose paints a picture of Lewis holed up in "his damp, chilly and smoky quarters, with only a candle for illumination." Even their supply of candles ran out on January 13, and they had to use elk fat to make what Lewis termed "this necessary article."

There, sitting at his split-plank table, Lewis penned long, detailed descriptions of what they had seen on the Lower Columbia. He wrote extensively about the botany, zoology, geography, and particularly, the ethnology of the area, and his writing and illustrations contributed greatly to increased contemporary knowledge. He described ten newly discovered plants and trees in great detail and collected dozens of plants, leaves, and cones. In total, he wrote about 100 animals—thirty-five mammals, fifty birds, ten reptiles and fish, and five invertebrates. Of these, twenty-four were new to science.

He wrote even more extensively about the local Indians. There were detailed descriptions of the various types of Indian canoes—something he greatly admired. He described their wooden houses and their sleeping mats, bowls, knives, bags, digging sticks, and clothing found within the dwellings. He particularly admired their wide-brimmed woven conical hats that deflected the ever-present rain.

But while Lewis and Clark enjoyed good relations with a few individual Indians, they ran into problems with their personal prejudices when they described the characteristics of the Indians as a group. These Indians simply didn't match their stereotypes of how Indian peoples should look or act. In addition, the restrictive visiting policy they created, the nightly curfew, and their unwillingness to visit nearby villages meant that they had fewer Indian informants. For those reasons, their "Estimate of the Western Indians," which Lewis prepared for Jefferson, is a much less successful ethnologic study than the "Estimate of the Eastern Indians" that had been written a year earlier.

While Lewis was occupied with his writing, Clark updated and improved his map. He completed it on February 11. Geographer John Logan Allen called it "the most important product of their winter on the Pacific." It was a collaborative effort. Lewis concluded that they had "found the most practicable and navigable passage across the Continent of North America." But that comment was probably tinged with a sense of disappointment. They had failed to find an all-water route to the Pacific. It didn't exist.

The good news was that land route they *had* discovered was made practical by the availability of horses on both sides of the Continental Divide from tribes who had no direct trading relationships with the

British. Indeed, the captains concluded that the United States enjoyed a distinct competitive advantage when it came to the fur trade. While the British had to ship their furs from the Canadian wilderness to London before they could be sent on to China, the Americans—*if* they could establish a trading post at the mouth of the Columbia, and *if* they could get the furs from the interior to the river—could cut a full year off the time it took their British competitors to get their furs to the Orient.

But before they could transmit that important information, they had to get home. The captains were intent on making the return in one season. Lewis had said that he wanted to remain at Fort Clatsop until April 1, but he moved the departure date forward to March 20 or whenever the weather became calm enough not to strand them again on the log-strewn beaches of the Columbia estuary. They began to make preparations.

On March 6, Patrick Gass wrote that he was "employed in repairing the canoes." On the ninth, John Shields set to work fabricating waterproof elk skin bags to keep their documents and multiple collections dry. March 20 came and went with the same howling winds that had first greeted them at winter camp.

Lewis summarized their winter at Fort Clatsop:

> Altho' we have not fared sumptuously this winter and spring at Fort Clatsop, we have lived quite as comfortably as we had any reason to expect we should, and have accomplished every object which induced our remaining at the place except that of meeting with the traders who visit the entrance of this river.

Significant problems faced them on their return journey. They were almost out of trade goods. "Two handercheifs would not contain all the small articles of merchandise which we possess," Lewis wrote. The rest of their stock consisted of one uniform coat and a hat and five robes made out of pieces of their flag.

They would also need canoes. Fortunately, their prized Indian canoe—which had earlier been given up as lost when it had been improperly tied up during a storm—was discovered by accident in early March. On March 17, Lewis instructed Drouillard to sell his prized coat to pay for another Indian canoe. Finally, without enough trade goods remaining to pay for one, they resorted to stealing a third canoe. Lewis did not write about it in his journal, but Sergeant Ordway did on March 18.

> We yet want another canoe, and as the Clatsops will not sell us one at a price which we can afford to give we will take one of them in lue of the six Elk which they stole from us in the winter.

He conveniently forgot to mention that the Indians had paid for the stolen elk with dogs. Trading a rifle and some ammunition for a canoe would have been an easy option, but it would have violated one of Lewis and Clark's absolute rules about not providing guns to the natives.

Chief Coboway visited the fort on that same day, and the soldiers had to rush to hide the canoe from him. Lewis gave him lists of the men who had comprised the expedition and asked him to distribute them to the other local chiefs in case they came in contact with a trading ship. He posted another list on the door of his quarters. In an introduction he wrote:

> The object of this list is, that through the medium of some civilized person who may see the same, it may be made known to the informed world, that the party consisting of the persons [named], and who were sent out by the government of the U' States in May 1804 to explore the interior of the Continent of North America, did penetrate the same . . . [to] the Pacific Ocean where they arrived on the 14th November 1805, and from whence they departed the ___ day of March

1806 on their return to the United States by the same rout they had come out.

President Jefferson had hoped that the party might be able to contact a trading vessel when they reached the mouth of the Columbia and perhaps, using his blank letter of credit, buy passage back to America. No such vessel materialized during the winter of 1805–1806, although one did arrive soon after their departure. Even if one had materialized, Lewis had concluded that

> Our party are also too small to think of leaving any of them to return to the U' States by sea, particularly as we shall be necessarily divided into three or four parties on our return in order to accomplish the objects we have in view.

On March 22, as the winds began to die down, Lewis presented the local Chinook chief, Coboway, with "our houses and furniture." Ordway noted only that "the rain Seased and it became fair. About meridian at which time we loaded our canoes & at 1 P.M. left Fort Clatsop on our homeward bound journey."

An interesting postscript to their winter at Fort Clatsop occurred eight years later in 1814 when Coboway, still fondly remembering the "cloth men," brought the piece of paper that he had been given by Lewis and Clark to a trader for the British North West Company. Coboway had carefully preserved it for all those years. The chief was introduced to the world of imperial power politics when the trader threw the priceless document into the fire and wrote out a British replacement.

CHAPTER SEVEN

# Homeward Bound

THE PARTY THAT departed from Fort Clatsop on March 23, 1806, was a shadow of its former self. The men carried with them their rifles, powder and ball, scientific instruments, some food, cooking utensils, a few trade goods, and the clothes on their backs. After being cooped up for three-and-a-half months, however, they were united in their desire to head home.

Within an hour of leaving the fort, they encountered a band of Chinooks whose chief had a canoe he wanted to sell. "Being already supplied" with canoes (including the one they had stolen), Lewis declined to buy it. The next day, however, an Indian who was guiding them through the many islands on the south side of the Columbia estuary claimed that the stolen canoe was his. Outnumbered and outgunned, he accepted a dressed elk hide for it. They camped that night near the John Day River on the east side of what they called Pt. William (Tongue Point).

Despite the force of the spring runoff flowing down the Columbia, which made their ascent difficult, they made good progress during the early days of their return. They paddled and sometimes pulled the heavy dugout canoes upriver against the current, past the villages of the Cathlamets, the Wahkiakums, and the Multnomahs. Lewis continued to show a morbid fascination for the burial sites of the dead. On March 30, the group camped on the Washington side across from Hayden Island near the current city of Vancouver, Washington. On the thirty-first, they moved to a camp located just east of Washougal, Washington, where they stayed for six days.

It was here, on April 1, that Lewis received a party of Indians who had come down the river in search of food. With the start of the spring salmon run still a month off, they said that a "great scarcity of food" awaited them as they worked their way up the river. With considerable understatement, Lewis wrote that the information "gave us much uneasiness with respect to our future means of subsistence." In the Mid-Columbia shrub steppe, between The Dalles and the Nez Percé villages, there were few large game animals, and if the tribes had exhausted their supplies of food, they might not be able to purchase fish, or even tribal dogs, for food.

The next day Clark and seven men left to explore the Willamette River (which he called the Multnomah) as far as the current city of Portland, Oregon. He had heard about the river, but missed it during their previous descent. Lewis remained in camp, supervising the preparation of elk jerky for the trip and describing some newly found plants and animals, including the flowering dogwood, red current, gooseberry, wood duck, and California quail.

On April 6, they passed by the distinctive Rooster Rock on the south side of the river and camped for two nights below the current site of Shepperd's Dell State Natural Area. One night, a sentry detected an old Indian man trying to enter their campsite. He sent him off with a few "stripes with a switch," but it was the first time any of the party had whipped an Indian. The next day, during a stop at another village, Private John Colter found Private Charles Floyd's tomahawk, which had been stolen from him on their previous visit. Some Indians tried to reclaim it from him again, but Lewis wryly records that "he retained it." On the captain's orders, John Shields, their best gunsmith, repaired and sighted their rifles in preparation for the trip ahead.

The next day they passed by Bridal Veil and Multnomah Falls, where Lewis remarked on how the "beautiful cascades . . . fall from a great hight over stupendious rocks . . . the most remarkable of these cascades falls 300 feet perpendicularly over a solid rock into a narrow bottom of the river on the south side." They camped that night at an Indian village located just north of the Bonneville Dam on the south shore across from Bradford Island.

*"Past several beautiful cascades."*
*Credit: Oregon Historical Society*

On April 10 and 11, they camped below the Cascades of the Columbia at Bradford Island (Brant Island) near Bonneville Dam. The canoes had to be towed through the rapids by elk rope, and the men and supplies portaged 2,800 feet "along a narrow rough and slippery road," with much difficulty and resulting fatigue. Lewis wrote that "the water appears to be considerably upwards of 20 feet higher than when we descended the river."

He consoled himself with the thought that the volume of water in the river must mean that the snow was melting in the mountains. At least, with the good weather, there were spectacular views of both Mount St. Helens—still a perfect cone before its 1980 eruption—and Mount Hood.

But the arduous portage was not the only problem. Their confrontations with the local Indians continued. Lewis wrote that during their portage around the Cascades,

> Great numbers of the nativs visited us and viewed
> us from the banks as we passed on with the canoes,
> many of these people were also about our baggage and
> on the portage road. An Indian standing on a ledge
> threw some rocks at the soldiers laboring below.

Lewis added, "These are the greates thieves and scoundrels we have met with." That evening, three Indians tried to steal Lewis's dog, Seaman, throwing Lewis into another rage. He sent three men out with orders to retrieve the dog and to fire on them "if they made the least resistence or difficulty in surrendering the dog." Back at camp, another Indian tried to steal an ax. Lewis warned them of "instant death" if any further attempts to steal their property were made. To complicate matters even more, one of the large dugout canoes was swept away on the following day, although Lewis was able to replace it with two small Indian canoes at the cost of "two robes and four elkskins."

Finally above the Cascades, they stopped for three days (April 15 to 18) at their previous Fort Rock campsite at The Dalles to prepare for their next great test, the Long Narrows. The site was now crowded with Indians who were gathering in anticipation of the spring salmon run. Given the condition of the river, they decided to abandon their canoes and proceed on horseback to the mouth of the Snake.

But first, they had to purchase the horses they needed, and they had precious little to offer for them. Clark went ahead to a village at the current site of Dallesport, but the Indians there were unwilling to trade. He proceeded along the well-worn trail (some of which is still visible) to the historic Wishram trading village of Nixluidix in the hope of acquiring at least five horses. Again, the Indians were unwilling to sell their horses for what the destitute explorers were prepared to pay.

Finally, Lewis had no choice but to authorize the payment of two large kettles for four horses, one of which promptly ran off after a soldier failed to hobble it properly. Lewis lost his temper again. "This in addition to the other difficulties under which I labored was truly provoking."

*Wishram community, also known as Nixluidix*
*(Wakemap mound, far left center. Celilo Falls below hills, far right).*
*Credit: Oregon Historical Society*

They camped for two more days at the site of their former camp at Horsethief Lake State Park at the upper end of the Long Narrows, where Lewis recorded that they "employed all hands in transporting our baggage on their backs and by means of the four pack-horses over the portage." While they were there, on April 19, the explorers celebrated the arrival of the spring salmon with the local natives.

But even in the excitement surrounding the arrival of the salmon, the Indian problems continued. The captains decided to burn their canoes arty, while camping at Wishram on April 21, in preparation for leaving the area by horseback. Lewis did not want to leave anything that would benefit the Indians. When an Indian tried to retrieve an iron socket from a canoe paddle that remained after the fire, Lewis lost his composure, beat the man, and had the rest of his men kick him out of camp.

The next morning, Charbonneau's saddle and a robe were missing. Lewis threatened to "birn their houses" if the items were not found. Fortunately, they were recovered after a search of the lodges. No villages were burned; no Indians were shot, but there has since been plenty of conjecture as to whether Meriwether Lewis was in full control of his emotions.

Finally beyond the Narrows, the party marched east through rocky country high along the northern bank of the river, past what is now the Maryhill Museum. The march was made more difficult as a result of too few horses and too many sore feet and twisted ankles experienced by men not used to marching.

Six days later the party camped on the Washington side at Plymouth, just below today's McNary Dam, where they were met by Chief Yelleppit and six Walla Wallas who escorted them to their village on the river opposite the mouth of the Walla Walla River. During their previous visit, in October 1805, they had promised that they would stay with him for several days on their return journey, and now he offered them food and horses.

On April 28, the chief surprised Clark with the gift of "a very elegant white horse" but then asked for a large kettle in return. With no large kettles remaining, Clark gave him his sword, powder, and 100 balls of ammunition. They received two more horses from lesser chiefs, which cost Lewis one of his matched pair of dueling pistols.

But the most important thing they received from the Walla Wallas was information. Again good fortune shone on them. A captive Shoshone woman lived with the tribe. She could converse freely with Sacajawea, who passed the information on to her husband, who then passed it on to Drouillard, who could repeat it in English to the captains. They learned of an overland shortcut that generally paralleled the southern side of the Snake River through rolling hills to the current town of Dayton, Washington, and then east along the northeast branch of Petit Creek to a point near the junction of the Snake and the Clearwater, saving eighty miles.

The group remained with Yelleppit an extra day while he hosted a feast and dance for the visitors, to which members of other local tribes had been invited in large numbers. There was a long night of farewell festivities.

The morning of April 30, they crossed the Columbia and left with twenty-three horses to follow the overland trail that Yelleppit had suggested. In his journal, Lewis paid the Walla Wallas a supreme compliment when he called them "the most hospitable, honest, and sincere people that we have met with on our voyage."

After a four-day march that included wind, rain, and snow, they were met on the afternoon of May 4 by a party of Nez Percé led by Chief Tetoharsky, who with Twisted Hair had accompanied them as far as The Dalles the previous fall. The next day, Tetoharsky led them to the camp of an even more important Nez Percé chief named Cut Nose. He was one of the four principal chiefs of the area, and his mat lodge measured 15 by 156 feet. He had been off hunting when Lewis and Clark arrived the year before.

With the chiefs leading them, they arrived on the south side of the Snake River approximately seven miles west of its confluence with the Clearwater. They were back at the same place they had left on October 10 on their way to the Columbia and beyond. After camping at the junction for several days, the party crossed the Clearwater and following it to what is now Lenore, Idaho. Here, they climbed the steep canyon walls to camp on the broad plain above.

On May 8, they arrived at Twisted Hair's village, only to find themselves in the middle of what apparently had been a long-festering feud between Cut Nose and Twisted Hair about the latter's care of the horses they had left with him the year before. Cut Nose accused Twisted Hair of letting his young men ride and abuse the white men's horses. The Nez Percé Indians *were* notoriously hard on their horses because they owned so many of them, but Cut Nose might also have been jealous of Twisted Hair's close friendship with the captains.

And, although relations with the Nez Percé were generally excellent, there was yet another incident that suggests the stress of the expedition was getting to Lewis. The Nez Percé never ate dog and often made fun of the whites for doing so. One evening an Indian, mocking Lewis's preference for the animal, threw a half-starved puppy toward Lewis's plate. The captain caught it in mid-air and flung it back in the Indian's face with great force, grabbing his tomahawk as he rose in anger and indicating "by signs if he repeated his insolence I would tomahawk him."

The bad blood between Cut Nose and Twisted Hair was a potential impediment to Lewis and Clark's goal of uniting the Nez Percé as American allies in any future fur trade enterprise, so they met independently with each chief and negotiated a truce between them. On May 9, they recovered twenty-one of their horses and about half of their saddles, along with the powder and ammunition they had buried the year before.

The snow in the mountains (and in their camp) tried the patience of the men who were eager to move on, but there was nothing they could do about it. Lewis wrote of "that icy barrier which seperates me from my friends and Country, from all which makes life exteemable.—patience, patience—"

With their tolerance waning with each passing day, the explorers camped near the Nez Percé at a place they called Camp Chopunnish near Kamiah, Idaho, from May 14 to June 10, 1806. They used the time to hold an important council with the principal Nez Percé chiefs to discuss the establishment of trading posts, promote intertribal peace, and discuss future visits to Washington, DC.

Lewis recorded that they used the occasion to impress the chiefs with the power and scientific advancement of the United States "by showing them the power of magnetism, the spy glass, compass, watch, and air gun and sundry other articles equally novel and incomprehensible to them." They felt they had succeeded when one important chief told them that they had "opened his ears to our councils and that our words had made his heart glad."

Clark provided medical care for members of the tribe in return for food and horses. The soldiers competed with their Nez Percé counterparts in games and athletic contests and freely consorted with the Nez Percé women.

*Site of Camp Chopunnish on the banks of the*
*Clearwater River near Kamiah, Idaho.*
*Credit: Oregon Historical Society*

The enforced delay also allowed them time to obtain accurate information about the large Blackfoot Confederation—mortal enemies of the Nez Percé who lived on the eastern slopes of the Rocky Mountains in Canada and Montana—whom they would almost surely encounter. Lewis also received more information about the overland route he planned to take between Traveler's Rest and the Great Falls. Their horse herd grew to more than sixty.

As May turned into June, each day's delay made the waiting even harder. By June 15, the explorers decided to move their camp to Weippe Prairie, where they had first met the Nez Percé a year before. Cut Nose sent word that two of his young men would guide the party as far as the Great Falls of the Missouri. When, by June 14, the promised guides had not arrived, Lewis made an ill-considered decision to proceed to Traveler's Rest without them. He rationalized his decision in his journal. "We have been detained near five weeks in consequence of the snows," he wrote, "a serious loss of time at this delighfull season for traveling."

Within a day they found themselves in snow eight to ten feet deep. "Here was winter with all its rigors," Lewis wrote on June 17. They decided to return while their horses were still strong. The decision dejected them all. "This is the first time since we have been on this long tour that we have ever been compelled to retreat or make a retrograde march."

Drouillard and a soldier were sent back to Cut Nose's camp with the unprecedented offer of an rifle for anyone who would agree to guide them to Traveler's Rest and two more rifles and ten horses for anyone who would guide them to the Great Falls of the Missouri. The inducement worked. A younger brother of Cut Nose and the two lesser chiefs who had sold the captains horses at Twisted Hair's camp arrived on June 23. The expedition left the next morning at first light.

The guides led them through the deep mountain snow. They ran out of meat and subsisted on bear grease and roots for several days, but whenever they came upon a place where the snow had melted, they found their trail. On June 29 they descended into today's Lolo Hot Springs, Montana, and went into camp. A day later they reached Traveler's Rest. They had marched 156 miles through mountains more than 6,000c feet tall in six days.

# CHAPTER EIGHT

# A Big Gamble Pays Off

AT THEIR CAMP back at The Dalles, the captains made the final decision to implement the audacious plan for their return journey, which they had first developed during the winter at Fort Clatsop. On their trip west, they had learned of other routes between the Missouri and the Columbia but had not been in a position to explore them. Locating them and determining the best route was one of the central objectives of the trip.

Their plan was intricate and complicated. From Traveler's Rest, Lewis and nine men would follow the direct overland route—up the Blackfoot River, over the Continental Divide, and down the Medicine River to the Great Falls of the Missouri. Three of the men would remain there to uncover the cache of supplies they had left and organize a portage around the falls. Meanwhile, Lewis and the remaining men would explore the Marias River to the north to determine the exact latitude of the northernmost tributary of the Missouri.

This was "of the highest national importance," and Lewis "determined to execute it at every hazard," even risking encounters with roving Blackfoot Indian war parties. Once that was accomplished, he would then proceed south to the mouth of the Marias, located east of the Great Falls, where he would meet the rest of his men coming downriver from the falls. Lewis's decision to explore the Marias and seek out the Blackfoot was the most daring decision of the whole expedition, and it nearly failed.

While Lewis set off to explore the Marias, Clark would head down the Bitterroot Valley until he located the trail to the Jefferson River, which had been described to him the year before, and proceed to the Three Forks of the Missouri. Once there, his party would recover the boats they had left there, then split paths.

Clark would explore the Yellowstone to its junction with the Missouri near the North Dakota border, while Sergeant Ordway's party would paddle north on the Jefferson until they came to the Great Falls. Then they would make the portage around the falls and meet Lewis below the falls at the mouth of the Marias.

*Routes of Lewis and Clark through Montana.*
*Credit: National Park Service*

Sergeant Prior and two men were assigned to go on an independent mission. While Clark's party paddled down the Jefferson, Prior was to take the rest of the horse herd and head east to the Mandan villages. Prior would carry a letter to the British North West Company trader, Hugh Henry, offering him a salary to work for the Americans and use his influence to convince the Sioux chiefs to ally themselves with the Americans and visit Washington, DC.

It was a bold plan. Splitting their already small party into five groups too far apart to help one another was more than risky. The captains were willing to accept the risk because it furthered their goals of finding a more direct overland route between the Missouri and the Columbia, brokering a peace between the warring tribes, and setting in motion plans for the start of an American fur trade empire.

As it turned out, the plan worked, but just barely. The captains parted company at Traveler's Rest on the morning of July 3. Lewis wrote, "I took leave of my worthy friend and companion Capt. Clark and the party that accompanied him." They were now so confident in their abilities that as they bid farewell, they simply said that they would see each other at the junction of the Missouri and the Yellowstone in five or six weeks. Their proposed rendezvous was 500 miles to the east. To get there, Lewis would travel 800 miles and Clark nearly 1,000 miles.

## The Route of Meriwether Lewis

Lewis's party, including the five Nez Percé guides and seventeen horses, proceeded up the Bitterroot and Clark Fork Rivers to the present site of Missoula, Montana. July 4 came and went without incident, except that the Indian guides left, saying that they were no longer needed because the trail was so well marked that even a white man could find it.

Lewis discovered the trail on July 6. But, hoping to find buffalo, he took another trail he had heard about that crossed the Continental Divide, at what is now known as Lewis and Clark Pass. To the east, the Great Plains spread out in front of him into seeming infinity. He was once more in American territory. His group found the Sun River and followed it to its mouth on July 11. The next day they arrived at their former camp at White Bear Island, at the western end of the portage around the Great Falls. Up to that point, the expedition had enjoyed an unbroken spell of good luck. Now, for Meriwether Lewis at least, that luck began to change.

An unseen raiding party ran off with seven of their horses. Drouillard went after them on July 12 but failed to return for three days. After reaching camp at White Bear Island, Lewis found that his cache of plant specimens had been ravished by the spring floods. All were lost. At least they had come upon the buffalo herds and were now enjoying the long-sought-after meat and using the leftover hides to make "bull boats" (round, tub-like boats with a frame of willow branches covered with buffalo hides) to navigate the Missouri after portaging around the falls.

Despite losing the horses, Lewis decided to continue with his plan to explore the Marias River, but with only Drouillard and the Field brothers accompanying him. The remaining men would make the portage around the falls and meet him downriver—when, and if, he returned from the north.

Lewis's small party left on July 16 and found the Marias River two days later without incident. They followed it for three more days, discovering from Lewis's daily celestial sightings that the river did not extend as far north as they had hoped. Frustrated, they named the location Camp Disappointment. They also detected increased signs of nearby Indian activity, so they turned south on July 26, hoping to avoid contact with what would probably be a Blackfoot war party.

Their change of direction was too late. That day they came upon a party of eight Piegan Blackfoot warriors intently watching Drouillard, who was scouting ahead of the rest of the party. Several were armed with British trade muskets. Trying to assume control of the situation, Lewis approached the surprised braves with a flag he had brought along for just this eventuality, offering them a smoke and some small medals.

Warily, they decided to camp together for the night. Using sign language, Lewis then made his patented trade and peace speech but made the mistake of telling them that he had been organizing their enemies, the Nez Percé and the Shoshones, in a trading alliance and that their access to British guns would soon be ended. As historian James Ronda described it, "The clash of empires had come to the Blackfeet."

In the early morning hours of July 27, Lewis was awakened by the sound of Drouillard shouting, "Damn you, let go my gun," while fighting with an Indian who was trying to steal his gun. Lewis's rifle was already missing. In the ensuing melee, Reuben Fields killed one of the Indians with his knife, and Lewis shot another in the stomach while barely missing being shot himself. "I felt the wind of his bullet very distinctly."

They recovered four of their own horses, took four of the remaining Indian horses, and left camp immediately. Off they rode on a "beautiful level plain" toward the junction of the Marias and the Missouri just as quickly as their horses would carry them.

On July 28, the party finally came to a stop on the banks of the Missouri after a forced ride of more than 100 miles that took them almost twenty-four hours to complete. Within hours they "heared the report of several rifles very distinctly . . . we quickly repared to this joyfull sound and on arriving at the bank of the river had the unspeakable satisfaction to see our canoes coming down." Lewis and his party released the horses, joined Ordway and the others in the boats, and paddled down the river in haste.

On August 7, they came to the mouth of the Yellowstone, where they had planned to meet Clark, but he was not there. He left a note saying he had gone on because the game was scarce and the mosquitoes plentiful in that location. Lewis followed him downriver.

On the eleventh, seeing some elk on shore, Lewis landed his boat to replenish their meat supply. Charging into the willows along the bank, Lewis killed an elk while Private Cruzatte wounded another. Lewis was about to take aim on a third when he was shot in the buttocks. "Damn you. You have shot me," Lewis yelled at the invisible, but nearsighted, Cruzatte.

There was no answer. Could an Indian have shot him? Was Cruzatte alive? Bleeding from his wound, Lewis limped back to the boat to rally the rest of his men, now on high alert. They charged into the woods while Lewis laid himself out prone on the bottom of one of the canoes with his rifle and pistol at his side. He was determined to die bravely if that were his fate.

After about twenty minutes, the men returned with Cruzatte, who vehemently denied shooting his captain. But Lewis now had the proof—a ball from a .54 caliber 1803 model US Army rifle, a weapon no Indian would likely possess. The ball had entered and exited Lewis's buttocks and lodged against his tough elk-hide breeches.

Lewis, suffering, tended to his wound as they continued down the Missouri in search of Clark. Instead, they found another note. Bad news. Sergeant Pryor and his men had rejoined Clark's party after the horses they were taking to the Mandans were stolen by Crow Indians only a day into their mission. The horses, which were worth money needed to buy supplies, were gone, and so was any hope of contacting Hugh Haney and having him intercede with the Sioux. Unfazed, Pryor and his men shot some buffalo and built two bull boats, which they used to float down the Yellowstone until they found Clark on August 8.

By now, Lewis was running a high fever and had the wound treated with a poultice of Peruvian bark until he was well enough to continue. The fever receded, but the pain did not.

## The Route of William Clark

Clark left Traveler's Rest on July 3 with Charbonneau and his family, York, and ten men. They headed up the Bitterroot Valley until they found the trail to the Jefferson River that Clark had heard about the year before. For the first time, Sacajawea actively served as guide. On July 6, Clark recorded, "The Indian woman informed me that she had been in this plain frequently and knew it well." This is known today as Gibbons Pass, Montana.

On July 8, they reached Camp Fortunate, where they had buried some canoes and supplies, including tobacco, the previous August. The men "became so impatient to be chewing [the tobacco] that they scarcely gave themselves time to take their saddles off their horses," Clark wrote.

They embarked in their canoes down the Jefferson River toward Three Forks, which they reached two days later, while Ordway followed along with the horse herd. Here, according to their plan, Clark split his party.

Ordway paddled north, aided by the Missouri River current, to the agreed-on rendezvous with Lewis at Great Bear Island. There, Ordway used their horses to pull the boats, including the larger white pirogue, over the portage around the Great Falls in eight days. It had taken them a month the year before. They then headed downstream, where they encountered Lewis returning from the Marias on July 27.

Clark took eight men, Charbonneau and his family, and York and set out overland for the Yellowstone. On July 13, Sacagawea, still guiding Clark through lands familiar to her, advised Clark to cross into the Yellowstone River basin by what is now known as Bozeman Pass. They reached the Yellowstone two days later. Clark became the first white man to view what today is Yellowstone National Park.

As soon as he found some suitable cottonwood trees, he fashioned two dugout canoes and lashed them together for increased stability. On July 25, he carved his name on a block-like sandstone rock formation that he named Pompey's Pillar, for Sacajawea's son. They continued the journey and paddled through beautiful country filled with buffalo. They passed the mouth of the Rosebud on the twenty-eighth, the Powder on the twenty-ninth, and finally reached the confluence of the Yellowstone and Missouri on August 3.

## Reunited Again

On August 11, while waiting for Lewis, Clark's party encountered two American trappers headed up the Yellowstone to trap beaver. The next day, to everyone's great relief and delight, Lewis's and Ordway's parties, now reunited, "hove into Sight" and landed at Clark's camp. Clark inspected Lewis's wound, which was finally starting to heal. Now the primary objective would be to reach St. Louis before the Missouri froze over.

Late in the afternoon the two American trappers again arrived in camp. They decided to travel with the soldiers to the Mandan villages, which they reached on August 14. "These people were extreamly pleased to see us," Clark wrote, but the news they provided was bad.

The Indians of the upper Missouri were at war. It was as if Lewis and Clark had never arrived. Nor were any of the chiefs willing to travel to Washington, DC, because of their fear of the Sioux.

On August 17, the captains paid Charbonneau "for his services... in all amounting to 500 dollars and 33 and a third cents." Sacajawea received nothing, although Clark offered to take her son, "a butifull promising child who is about 19 months old," and raise him as if he were his own boy. Charbonneau and Sacajawea asked Clark to wait a year until the boy was older. Private Coulter asked to be discharged to join the two American trappers and hunt beaver on the Yellowstone.

What remained of the Corps of Discovery stayed with the Mandans for three days, while the captains engaged in inconclusive negotiations to convince the Mandan chiefs to go with them to meet President Jefferson. One finally agreed after being persuaded by a French trapper, who demanded that Clark feed and transport his family in return for using his influence.

On August 31, they had another near run-in with the Teton Sioux, but refused their demands to stop. Six days later, they encountered another boatload of traders headed upriver. Lewis wrote that they purchased a gallon of whiskey, "the first Spiritous licqour which had been tasted by any of them Since the 4 of July 1805." They were making seventy to eighty miles a day with the current—past the Platte, past the Kansas, and meeting trading parties headed upriver every day. On September 4, they stopped to pay tribute to Sergeant Charles Floyd, who was the only man lost during the entire expedition.

They entered the Mississippi on a "wet and disagreeable morning—September 23, 1806." Clark wrote that they "descended to the Mississippi and down that river to St. Louis at which place we arrived about 12 oClock. We Suffered the party to fire off their pieces as a Salute to the Town." They were home.

The independent explorations of the Yellowstone and the Marias Rivers that they had undertaken during their return had been risky, even foolhardy, but had resulted in valuable information. Lewis's trip confirmed what they previously only assumed. The best route to the Columbia was to leave the Missouri at the Great Falls and head west on the Nez Percé buffalo road. Clark's exploration proved that the route along the Yellowstone was easy but increased the length of the trip. The route they had traveled in 1805 was the best. The distance from the Mississippi, up the Missouri, and on to the Pacific Ocean was 3,555 miles.

# In the Wake of Lewis and Clark

THE TITLE OF this book is something of a double entendre. As its first meaning, it refers to the fact that your ship follows the route taken by Lewis and Clark and the Corps of Discovery up and down the Snake and Columbia Rivers. As used again as the title for this chapter, it refers to the later lives of the major participants and the tremendous economic, demographic, geopolitical, and scientific changes that resulted from Lewis and Clark's exploration, starting with the captains themselves.

## Meriwether Lewis

On the day following his arrival at St. Louis, Meriwether Lewis began writing a long letter to his friend and mentor, President Thomas Jefferson, holding up the eastern mail until he had finished. He began by telling Jefferson that they had arrived safely in St. Louis with "our papers and baggage." His second sentence provided the most significant news. They had "penetrated the Continent of North America to the Pacific Ocean, and sufficiently explored the interior . . . to affirm with confidence that we have discovered the most practicable rout which does exist across the continent."

He went on to say that the navigation of the Missouri River, and also that of the Clearwater, Snake, and Columbia Rivers, was good, at least as far as The Dalles, and that small ships could sail from the mouth of the Columbia to that point. The overland route from the Missouri to the Clearwater was 340 miles—200 of it along a good trail, but the remaining 140 miles through "tremendious mountains which for 60 mls. Are covered with eternal snows."

He described his grand design for the creation of an American fur trade empire that involved collecting furs from the entire inland northwest and transporting them by horse and boat to the mouth of the Columbia, where they would be shipped to Canton and exchanged for trade goods desired by the American market. It was designed to completely eliminate the British competition. "Many articles not bulky . . . [or] of a very perishable nature may be conveyed to the United States . . . without having to sail half way around the world by way of the Cape of Good Hope."

He noted that his plan would require considerable expense and an expanded military to protect the trade routes, something Jefferson was probably not happy to hear. Lewis said that he would be in Washington shortly to provide the president with additional details and bring Clark's map, which "I am unwilling to wrisk by the Mail."

The press reports of the party's return, many initiated by Lewis himself, created a firestorm of interest, particularly among investors and entrepreneurs wanting to get in on the ground floor of the fur trade. Everywhere he went he was overwhelmed by the questions and adulation of enthusiastic crowds.

While Jefferson waited for him in Washington and at Monticello, Lewis remained in St. Louis, trying to settle the bills remaining from the expedition. They held a public auction and sold all the items that had survived the trip, including rifles, powder horns, and axes. They brought in $408.62.

Lewis's long letter reached Jefferson on October 24. He responded immediately, urging Lewis to come to Monticello. Lewis and Clark left St. Louis in early November with an entourage that included Big White, the Mandan chief, and several other members of the expedition. They arrived at Charlottesville on December 13 and at Washington, DC, on December 28, 1806, where Lewis promoted his vision of an American fur trading empire at every opportunity.

Lewis stayed with Jefferson through the winter months, and it was during this time that his personal life began to fall apart. Over Lewis's objections, the War Department refused to make Clark's temporary rank of captain permanent. And while payments and land grants were authorized for all members of the expedition, except Sacajawea and York, Clark received a smaller land grant than Lewis.

The expedition had cost a great deal more than anticipated, and while Jefferson never complained, many others, including John Adams and the Federalists, did. It took Congress almost a month to approve compensation for the members of the expedition. In 1807, Jefferson appointed Lewis as governor of the Louisiana Territory, while Clark's promotion to lieutenant colonel in the regular army was overlooked.

In Philadelphia, Lewis worked with collaborators to prepare his journal for publication. In the meantime, he was still fighting with the accountants at the War Department about his expenditures during and after the expedition. The bills totaled $38,722.25. Jefferson was beginning to have second thoughts about the wisdom of appointing Lewis as governor. Although Jefferson wanted him to get the journals published, Lewis was still in Philadelphia instead of St. Louis, where things were falling apart in his absence.

In the meantime, Lewis's fame weighed on him. He began to drink heavily. Always a hypochondriac, Lewis began taking opiates and other medicines. He promised Jefferson that he would leave for St. Louis and his official duties in July 1807, but he didn't actually depart until the winter of 1808. Meanwhile, he paid little attention to what was going on there.

When he finally arrived in St. Louis, he plunged into his duties with a vengeance. He lobbied to have the British North West Company excluded completely from the Louisiana Territory when tensions between the United States and Great Britain rose after the "Chesapeake Affair," in which the Royal Navy's HMS *Leopard* fired several broadsides into a newly commissioned American ship after she refused to allow the British to board and search for British crewmen.

As governor, Lewis published the first laws in the Upper-Louisiana Territory. He built new roads. His efforts to negotiate peace among the quarrelling tribes and his duty to enforce Indian treaties were less than successful and triggered endless conflict among the government and the tribes as a flood of trappers and settlers looked to open new lands. He was also involved in a series of highly controversial conflicts about trading licenses, land grant politics, and his Indian policy, particularly with territorial secretary Frederick Bates, who attempted to undermine the vulnerable Lewis at every turn and instead promote himself as governor.

With relatively little experience in politics and government, Lewis's actions and remoteness even led Jefferson to complain that "Since I parted with you in Albemarle [Sound] in Sept. last I have never had a line from you." What confounded Jefferson even more was the fact that Lewis had not yet penned the first lines of his much anticipated book.

Instead, Lewis busied himself organizing the Missouri River Fur Company with Clark and prominent St. Louis businessmen as partners. As Stephen Ambrose has written, "The scheme smacked of nepotism and reeked of conflict of interest."

He decided to raise a local militia to return Big White—still in St. Louis—to his Mandan village. Based largely on Frederick Bates's accusations, the War Department refused to reimburse Lewis for the $7,000 he had borrowed from others to raise the militia. When his creditors heard that he would not be reimbursed, they called his debts, forcing him to liquidate his assets, including the land he had been granted for his part in the expedition. It was bad enough that Jefferson was unhappy with him, but now there was a new president, James Madison, in the White House, and he saw Lewis in a exceedingly different light.

Drinking heavily, in poor health, and broke, Lewis decided to journey to Washington to confront his critics and clear his name. On October 9, he reached Grinder's Inn, a rural, log cabin stop located along the historic Natchez Trace highway, ninety miles southwest of

Nashville. Unstable, sick, and drunk, he shot himself in the middle of the night.

Stephen Ambrose best summed up the life of Meriwether Lewis when he wrote in *Undaunted Courage*:

> As a man, he was full of contradictions. He had been a curious, active boy; a hard-drinking, hard riding army officer; an intensely partisan secretary to the president; and eager explorer; a scientific scholar who paid close attention to detail; a Philadelphia playboy; an overeager governor and speculator in land; a drug taker and an alcoholic.
>
> But he was a great company commander, the greatest of all American explorers, and in the top rank of world explorers.

## William Clark

William Clark returned to Clarksville, Tennessee, and the home of his older brother, George Rogers Clark, after his return from the Pacific. In 1807, after being denied his commission in the regular army, President Jefferson appointed Clark as brigadier general of the Louisiana territorial militia and Indian affairs agent, after his promotion to lieutenant colonel was blocked by the War Department.

Headquartered in St. Louis, Clark regularly consulted with Lewis about their Indian policies and the publication of their journals. They remained close friends, and it must have been difficult for Clark to witness his friend's increasing difficulties. He had agreed to meet Lewis in Washington, DC, on Lewis's final trip, but they traveled by different routes. He could not have been surprised when he learned about his friend's apparent suicide.

With Lewis gone, the responsibility of publishing the journals fell to Clark. After several attempts, he finally selected a twenty-six-year-old child prodigy, Nicholas Biddle, to edit the journals. Clark and others helped Biddle, but the project was jinxed. Dr. Benjamin Barton was retained to write the scientific volume that would accompany Biddle's two-volume narrative, but his health failed and he could not complete his work. The War of 1812 started just as Biddle was ready to turn over his manuscript to the publisher, and then the publishing house collapsed. Biddle's work did not appear until 1814.

*William Clark's map published by Nicholas Biddle in 1814.*
*Credit: Library of Congress*

Clark married Julia Hancock on January 5, 1808, at Fincastle, Virginia. He reportedly first met her as a fourteen-year-old teenager before he left for the west. He must have thought of her along the way, because when he returned, he asked her to marry him. They had five children, including their firstborn, a boy, named Meriwether Lewis Clark in honor of his friend and co-leader of the Corps of Discovery.

Julia died at the age of twenty-nine in 1820, leaving Clark a single father of five small children. Later that year, he married Harriet Kennerly Radford, a widow and Julia's first cousin, whom he had met while courting Hancock. They had three children together, of whom two survived, before she died suddenly on Christmas Day, 1831.

In 1809, President Madison appointed Clark as the governor of the Louisiana (and later, the Missouri) Territory and de-facto superintendent of Indian affairs. Indian diplomacy occupied much of his time. He again saw active military service along the Mississippi during the War of 1812. He was reappointed by Madison in 1816 and again by President James Monroe in 1820.

When Missouri became a state in 1820, Clark ran for governor but was defeated. In 1822, Monroe appointed him to the newly created position of superintendent of Indian affairs. Even though Clark was a strong supporter of Indian culture, language, and history, he did not fail to have them removed from their lands, while encouraging federal efforts to assimilate, educate, and civilize them. Clark died on September 1, 1838.

## Other Members of the Expedition

Several of the soldiers of the expedition went on to lead memorable lives. Sergeant Patrick Gass returned to the army and lost an eye in the War of 1812. He settled in Wellsberg, West Virginia, where he married Maria Hamilton and fathered seven children. He died in 1870 at the age of ninety-nine.

Sergeant Nathaniel Pryor also returned to the army and fought at the Battle of New Orleans in the War of 1812. Pryor traded on the Arkansas River and married an Osage woman. He lived with the tribe until his death in 1831.

John Coulter returned to the Rockies as a trapper for four years, becoming one of the best-known early mountain men. He was the first white to report on the geysers at what became Yellowstone National Park. Colter married and settled in Missouri, where he died in 1813.

William Clark eventually granted his African-American slave, York, freedom when the resumption of servitude became unbearable for York after the freedom he had enjoyed during the expedition. Clark set him up in a freight-hauling business between Nashville, Tennessee, and Richmond, Virginia, giving him a wagon and six horses. The writer, Washington Irving, who once interviewed Clark in 1832, recorded that York's venture failed and he tried to return to Clark's service. He told Irving that "He . . . set off for St. Louis, but was taken with cholera in Tennessee & died."

President Thomas Jefferson served as president of the United States from March 4, 1801, to March 4, 1809. In his last years in the White House, he lost confidence in Lewis but refrained from criticizing him in public. He remained on friendly terms with Clark, who continued to send him animal fossils and small bones from the west that he thought the president might enjoy. He did, keeping a special room full of them at the White House.

When Jefferson heard of Lewis's death, only two months after he left office, he—like Clark—believed it to be suicide and made no public comment at the time.

After completing his second term as president, Jefferson retired to his mountaintop home at Monticello. Already a unique residence in many ways, Monticello housed the mounted animal heads, fossils, and Indian artifacts that Lewis and Clark had sent Jefferson.

## Thomas Jefferson

Jefferson went on to found the University of Virginia when he was seventy-six and donated his extensive library to the Library of Congress. At eighty-one, he hosted the Marquis de Lafayette at Monticello during Lafayette's triumphant return to America. Jefferson's health began to fail in 1825. He died on July 4, 1826, at the age of eighty-three, on the fiftieth anniversary of the Declaration of Independence; it was only a few hours before the death of his longtime political opponent, John Adams. The two men had renewed their friendship in their final years.

## Sacajawea

For someone we know little about, there are probably more statues of Sacajawea, the Shoshone woman who traveled with Lewis and Clark to the Pacific and back, than any other American woman. It is said that she was born near the present-day town of Salmon in

Lemhi County, Idaho, about 1788. She and several other girls were kidnapped by a Hidatsa war party that took the girls to their village in North Dakota. Sacajawea was about twelve.

Sometime in 1801, she was taken as wife by Toussant Charbonneau, a French-Canadian trapper who lived with the Hidatsa. He had either purchased her from the Indians or perhaps won her while gambling. She was pregnant with their first child when Lewis and Clark wintered at Fort Mandan from 1804–1805.

The captains were looking for an interpreter and agreed to hire Charbonneau when they discovered that his wife spoke Shoshone. Her son, Jean Baptist Charbonneau, was born at Fort Mandan on February 11, 1805. Unlike Lewis, who once referred to her as a "squaw," Clark seem to genuinely like her, calling her "Janey." He took a particular liking to her son, calling the boy "Little Pomp" or "Pompy."

After their return from the Pacific, Charbonneau and Sacajawea spent three years living among the Hidatsa before accepting William Clark's invitation to settle in St. Louis. Fulfilling an earlier promise, Clark assumed responsibility for Pomp's education and sent him to a St. Louis boarding school. Sometime after 1810, Sacajawea gave birth to another child, a girl, while she and Charbonneau were living at the Fort Manuel Lisa Trading Post. Operated by the Missouri Fur Company, the trading post had been formed two years earlier by Lewis and Clark and others. She died there in 1812, at the age of twenty-five from "bilious fever." Charbonneau signed over custody of "Pomp" and his baby daughter to Clark the following year.

Sacajawea's son, Jean-Baptiste Charbonneau, lived a restless and adventurous life. Raised in St. Louis by Clark, he was befriended by a German prince and taken to Europe when he was eighteen. He spent six years living with European royalty, learned four languages, and fathered a son. He returned from Europe in 1829 to live a life hardly less exciting than his father's. He became a gold miner; a hotel clerk in Auburn, California; a guide for a group of Mormons headed to California; and a judge at the Mission San Luis Rey de Francia prior to California statehood. He died on May 16, 1866, of pneumonia at the age of sixty-one in Danner, Oregon. He was on his way to pan for gold in Montana.

## Native Americans

The fate of the American Indians that Lewis and Clark encountered during their expedition is one of the great American tragedies of the nineteenth and twentieth centuries. They were the inevitable victims of the widely held belief in American exceptionalism and its "Manifest Destiny," as the young nation swept all before it to advance across the North American continent, just as Jefferson had foreseen.

The Mandan Indians became famous through the paintings of George Catlin, who visited the Mandan villages in 1833. The tribe was nearly wiped out by a smallpox epidemic in 1837 and 1838. Under the Indian Reorganization Act of 1934, the Mandans were merged with the Hidatsa and Arikara tribes and assigned to the Fort Berthold Reservation in western North Dakota.

The Great Sioux Nation, consisting of three distinct groups and seven related tribes, posed the greatest threat to the westward expansion of the United States. Just as they had tried to block Lewis and Clark from coming up the Missouri, they fought valiantly to check the ever-growing pressure of American agricultural, mining, and business interests from occupying their homeland. They fought four wars with the US Army from 1862 to 1890. Today, they occupy numerous reservations in North Dakota, South Dakota, and Nebraska.

The Shoshone (or Snake Indians as Lewis referred to them) lived in a wide area of the mountain west. They fought several short wars against the US Army during the 1860s and 1870s. Because they were so scattered, the Shoshone people now live on more than twenty reservations and colonies.

At the time of Lewis and Clark, approximately 12,000 Nez Percé occupied approximately seventeen million acres in Washington, Oregon, Montana, and Idaho. By 1900, the population of the tribe had declined to less than 2,000. Unlike many of the other western tribes, the Nez Percé remained on friendly terms with the Americans until the tribe split over the issue of assimilation in the 1870s.

One faction, led by Lawyer, Twisted Hair's son, accepted assimilation. Another faction, led by Chief Joseph, decided to fight the Army in an attempt to escape to Canada. Their epic retreat is one of the great sagas of western Indian lore. Today, approximately 18,000 tribal members live on the 1,200-square-mile Nez Percé Indian Reservation in north-central Idaho. But not Joseph's band. They were considered too dangerous to be reunited with the rest of the tribe and were sent to the Colville Indian Reservation in north central Washington.

Chief Yellippit of the Walla Walla tribe befriended the Lewis and Clark expedition both on their way to, and their return from, the Pacific. It would be eighteen more years, though, before the tribe would establish long-term trading relationships with the Americans.

In the meantime, they found themselves embroiled in the British–American fur trade conflict. By 1810, David Thompson, a highly capable explorer/fur trader for the British North West Company, determined that Mackenzie had not, in fact, discovered the northernmost headwaters of the Columbia River. He determined to do so himself and establish British rights to the land north of the Columbia River.

Thompson arrived at the junction of the Snake and the Columbia on July 9, 1811, planting a pole in the ground and claiming the land for Great Britain. After a visit to the Americans at Fort Astoria, Thompson convinced Yelleppit that the Americans had not discovered the true headwaters of the Columbia, and they should, therefore, be prohibited from trading north of the Snake River.

Yelleppit received Thompson as a friend, just as he had Lewis and Clark. He encouraged him to build a trading post near the mouth of the Walla Walla River. The project was delayed until 1818, when Fort Nez Percé opened. Its name was later changed to Fort Walla Walla by the Americans. Today, more than 3,000 Walla Wallas, Umatillas, and Cayuse occupy the 271-square-mile Umatilla Indian Reservation located near Pendleton, Oregon.

The Wishram and Wasco Indians were decimated by disease during the nineteenth century. They were both forced to cede their tribal land to the Americans under 1855 treaties. The Wascos wound up living with the Warm Springs Indians and a band of Northern Paiute Indians (relatives of the Shoshone) on the 1,019-square-mile Warm Springs Indian Reservation in north-central Oregon. The Wishram Indians were relocated, under the treaty of 1855, to the 2,186-square-mile Yakima Indian Reservation, along with the larger Yakama tribe and a number of other, smaller bands.

The once numerous Chinook bands of the lower Columbia were also devastated by disease after the arrival of the white traders and settlers. They were briefly granted tribal status in 2001, but the recognition was withdrawn a year later. Today, the 2,700 tribal members generally live in the towns and cities in southwestern Washington.

## Fur Traders and Mountain Men

Meriwether Lewis's vision for an American fur trade empire began to be implemented even before the explorers returned to St. Louis. On August 11, Clark encountered two American trappers who were headed up the Yellowstone. They had left St. Louis only months after the departure of Lewis and Clark in 1804. But interest in the fur trade really expanded after reports of untold millions of beaver and otter, and equally untold profits, appeared in the national press following their return.

Starting as early as the 1530s, French explorers had traded for beaver pelts with native peoples in the Arctic and in eastern Canada. From 1660 until the end of the Seven Years' War in 1763, France and Great Britain fought each other for control of what is now Canada, while both sought to expand their fur trading territories. After the United States declared its independence, the British began to shift their fur trading efforts west, resulting in Mackenzie's and later Thompson's expeditions. One of Lewis and Clark's primary goals was to claim the region west of the Louisiana Territory for the United States, so that they could block the efforts of the British Hudson's Bay and North West Companies.

In 1808, a German refugee, John Jacob Astor, formed the American Fur Company in New York City. Following the grand plan suggested by Meriwether Lewis, he established a trading post at Astoria and resupplied it yearly by supply ship from New York. Those ships could then transport the furs that had been collected from the interior to China.

The competing British and American fur companies outbid each other to hire the most experienced and successful mountain men, including several, such as John Coulter and George Drouillard, who had been with the Lewis and Clark expedition.

During the War of 1812, Astor was forced to sell his trading posts in the Pacific Northwest to the North West Company. Following the war, however, the United States passed a law excluding foreign traders from operating on US territory, which freed Astor's company from having to compete with the British. Sensing the eventual decline of fur's popularity in men's hats in favor of silk, Astor withdrew from the company in 1834. Without his business acumen, the American Fur Company closed its doors in 1847.

In 1821, armed hostilities broke out between the British North West Company and the Hudson's Bay Company (HBC). The British government forced them to merge, and, in 1824, the HBC developed a number of farms and trading posts in the disputed territory. It established its headquarters at Fort Vancouver at what is now Vancouver, Washington, on land that it hoped would eventually be British.

## Westward Expansion

As the furs dwindled, settlers flooded the Pacific Northwest. The Oregon Trail, discovered and developed by trappers and mountain men between 1811 and 1840, was a 2,200-mile wagon trail that connected the state of Missouri to the Willamette Valley in Oregon. Lewis and Clark had mapped both ends of the trail, but it remained for the mountain men and early immigrants to discover South Pass, Wyoming, and build a lower and easier-to-navigate wagon road leading to the Snake.

The first large wagon train, consisting of 700 to 1,000 hardy travelers, arrived in Oregon via the new route in 1843. In 1846, a road around Mount Hood was completed, and thousands of American settlers flooded into the Willamette Valley. Between 1836 and 1869, approximately 400,000 travelers walked and rode over the trail in search of land and a better life. While Oregon was their primary destination, other new trails led to California and Utah.

When Thomas Jefferson had become president in March 1801, the great monarchial empires of Europe still fought with one another in what is broadly referred to as the Napoleonic Wars. The infant United States tried to remain out of their way but was unable to avoid deprivations against its citizens, particularly sailors, by Britain and France, not to mention Barbary pirates of North Africa.

Thomas Jefferson understood this world. He had served as US minister to France and as the nation's first secretary of state. He understood that America could not take its place among the great nations of the world until it gained control of the lands that stretched to the Pacific. Only then could America be protected by large oceans from European entanglements. It is from this perspective that we should look at the Louisiana Purchase and the Lewis and Clark expedition.

While the term "Manifest Destiny" was not coined by John L. O'Sullivan until the 1840s, Jefferson, Madison, and Jackson had all embraced the concept that the United States was pre-ordained to expand across the North American continent. Acquiring eastern

Canada was one of the factors behind the American's decision to go to war with Britain in 1812.

It was also one of the major rationales behind sending a US naval squadron—the United States Exploring Expedition—around the world between 1838 and 1842. In 1841, it arrived in Puget Sound to winter near the Hudson's Bay post at Fort Nisqually, south of current-day Tacoma, Washington. While primarily scientific in scope, the squadron's goals included looking for suitable naval bases in Puget Sound. It was the naval equivalent of the Lewis and Clark expedition.

The concept of Manifest Destiny was also the source of the cries of "Fifty-four Forty or Fight" by Henry Clay and, later, President James K. Polk. They claimed that the United States was entitled to the contested Oregon country that extended from Russian Alaska at 54°40' to the Mexican–California border at the 42nd parallel.

*Oregon boundary dispute, 1818–1846.*

But, while the fertile farming areas of southwest Washington and rich fishing and timber resources of Puget Sound were controlled by the Hudson's Bay Company, the British simply didn't have the resources to keep out the Americans. In fact, they needed them to farm their lands and work at their facilities.

Despite a show of force that included sending a squadron of British ships and Royal Marines to the San Juan Islands, Britain was simply not prepared to go to war over a region of diminishing importance. A compromise was concluded along the 49th parallel in 1846.

In 1846, the United States went to war with Mexico following its annexation of the Republic of Texas. As a result, it obtained California and the Mexican provinces north of the Rio Grande River. Texas was admitted to the union in 1845. Gold was discovered in California three years later, attracting thousands of miners, businessmen, and adventurers. A railroad was completed across the Isthmus of Panama in 1855, making it much easier for settlers to get to California and Puget Sound.

Iowa became a state in 1846, followed by Wisconsin in 1848. As a result of the influx of population following the Gold Rush and the availability of new gold for the federal treasury, California became a state in 1850 and Oregon followed nine years later. The first transcontinental railroad was completed in 1869. Washington, Montana, North Dakota, and South Dakota were admitted to the union in 1889, and Idaho joined them a year later.

Thomas Jefferson's vision of a nation that spanned the continent was realized in only forty years, and it began with Lewis and Clark.

# Bibliography

Allen, John Logan (1975). *Passage through the Garden: Lewis and Clark and the Image of the American Northwest.* Urbana: University of Illinois Press. ISBN 978-0-252-00397-4.

Ambrose, Stephen E. (1996). *Undaunted Courage: Meriwether Lewis, Thomas Jefferson, and the Opening of the American West.* New York: Simon and Schuster. ISBN 978-1-84739-763-8.

Ambrose, Stephen E.; Sam Abell (2002). *Lewis and Clark: Voyage of Discovery.* Roanoke, Virginia: National Geographic Society. ISBN 978-0-7922-6473-6.

Anderson, Fred (2000). *Crucible of War: The Seven Years' War and the Fate of Empire in British North America, 1754–1766.* New York: Knopf. ISBN 0-375-40642-5.

Bergon, Frank, ed. (1989). *The Journals of Lewis and Clark.* New York: Penguin Books. ISBN 978-0-14-243736-0.

Betts, Robert B. (2000). *In Search of York: The Slave Who Went to the Pacific with Lewis and Clark.* Boulder: University of Colorado Press. ISBN 978-0-87081-714-4.

Carriker, Robert C. (2005). *Ocian in View!, O! the Joy: Lewis and Clark in Washington State.* Tacoma: Washington State Historical Society. ISBN: 978-0-91704-873-9.

Clarke, Charles G. (1970). *The Men of the Lewis and Clark Expedition: A Biographical Roster of the Fifty-one Members and a Composite Diary of Their Activities from all Known Sources.* Glendale, California: A. H. Clark Co. ISBN 978-0-8032-6419-9.

Cook, Warren L. (1973). *Flood Tide of Empire: Spain and the Pacific Northwest, 1543–1819.* New Haven: Yale University Press. ISBN 0-300-01577-1.

Coues, Elliott, ed. (1987). *The History of the Lewis and Clark Expedition.* New York: Dover ed., 1987; reprint of 1893 Francis P. Harper, 4-vol. ed., 1893. ISBN 978-0-486-21268-5.

Cutright, Paul Russell (1976). *A History of the Lewis and Clark Journals.* Norman: University of Oklahoma Press. ISBN 978-0-8061-3247-1.

Cutright, Paul Russell (1989). *Lewis and Clark: Pioneering Naturalists.* Lincoln: University of Nebraska Press. ISBN 978-0-8032-6434-2.

Dattilio, Daniel (1986). *Fort Clatsop: The Story behind the Scenery.* Wickenberg, Arizona: KC Publications. ISBN 978-0-88714-011-2.

DeVoto, Bernard (1947). *Across the Wide Missouri.* New York: Houghton Mifflin. ISBN 0-395924-97-9.

DeVoto, Bernard (1998) [1952]. *The Course of Empire.* Boston: Houghton Mifflin Harcourt. ISBN 978-0-395-92498-3.

DeVoto, Bernard (April 30, 1997). *The Journals of Lewis and Clark* (Revised ed.). Boston: Mariner Books for Houghton Mifflin. ISBN 978-0-395-85996-4.

Dillon, Richard (1965). *Meriwether Lewis: A Biography.* New York: Coward-McCann. ISBN 0-944220-16-9.

Duncan, Dayton (1997). *Lewis and Clark: An Illustrated History*. New York: Knopf. ISBN 978-0-375-70652-3.

Duncan, Dayton (1988). *Out West: American Journey along the Lewis and Clark Trail*. New York: Penguin Books. ISBN 978-0-14-008362-0.

Duncan, Dayton; Ken Burns (1997). *Lewis and Clark: The Journey of the Corps of Discovery*. New York: Knopf. ISBN 0-679-45450-0.

Fanselow, Julie (1994). *The Traveler's Guide to the Lewis and Clark Trail*. Helena, Montana: Falcon Press. ISBN 978-1-56044-224-0.

Fanselow, Julie (2003). *Traveling the Lewis and Clark Trail*. Guilford, Connecticut: Globe Pequot Press. ISBN 978-0-7627-2589-2.

Ferris, Robert G.; Roy E. Appleman, eds. (1975). *Lewis and Clark: Historic Places Associated with Their Transcontinental Exploration (1804-06)*. Washington, DC: US Department of the Interior, National Park Service. ISBN 978-0-931056-09-3.

Fifer, Barbara; Vicky Soderberg (2002). *Along the Trail with Lewis and Clark*. Helena, Montana: Farcountry Press. ISBN 978-1-56037-188-5.

Furtwangler, Albert (1993). *Acts of Discovery: Visions of America in the Lewis and Clark Journals*. Urbana: University of Illinois Press. ISBN 0-252-06306-6.

Gragg, Rod. (2003). *Lewis and Clark on the Trail of Discovery: The Journey That Shaped America*. Nashville: Rutledge Hill Press. ISBN 978-1-401-60075-4.

Hawke, David Freeman (1980). *Those Tremendous Mountains: The Story of the Lewis and Clark Expedition*. New York: W. W. Norton Co. ISBN 978-0-393-31774-9.

Hunsaker, Joyce Badgley (2000). *Sacagawea Speaks: Beyond the Shining Mountains with Lewis and Clark*. Boise, Idaho: Tamarack Books. ISBN 978-1-58592-079-2.

Huser, Verne (2004). *On the River with Lewis and Clark*. College Station: Texas A&M University Press. ISBN 1-58544-320-4.

Jackson, Donald Dean (1979). *Letters of the Lewis and Clark Expedition, with Related Documents, 1783–1854*. Two volumes. Urbana: University of Illinois Press. ISBN 978-0-25-200697-5.

Jones, Landon Y., ed. (2000). *The Essential Lewis and Clark*. New York: Ecco Press. ISBN 978-0-06-019600-4.

Kubik, Barbara J. (1999) *Lewis and Clark: Voyage of Discovery in the Mid-Columbia River Region*. Tri-Cities, Washington: Tri-Cities Visitor and Convention Bureau. No ISBN number.

Lavender, David (1990). *The Way to the Western Sea: Lewis and Clark across the Continent*. New York: Anchor Books. ISBN 978-0-8032-8003-8.

Mansfield, Leslie (2002). *The Lewis and Clark Cookbook: Historic Recipes from the Corps of Discovery and Jefferson's America*. Berkeley: Celestial Arts. ISBN 978-1-58761-147-6.

Meacham, Jon (2012). *Thomas Jefferson: The Art of Power*. New York: Random House. ISBN 978-1-4000-6766-4.

Moulton, Gary E., ed. (1983–2001). *The Journals of the Lewis and Clark Expedition, Volumes 1–13*. Lincoln: University of Nebraska Press. ISBN 978-0-80322-9488.

Nicandri, David L. (2010). *River of Promise: Lewis and Clark on the Columbia*. Norman: University of Oklahoma Press. ISBN 978-0-98255-9710.

Patent, Dorothy Hinshaw (March 15, 2002). *Animals on the Trail with Lewis and Clark*. Illustrated by William Muñoz. New York: Clarion Books. ISBN 978-0-395-91415-1.

Patent, Dorothy Hinshaw (2003). *Plants on the Trail with Lewis and Clark*. Photography by William Muñoz. New York: Clarion Books. ISBN 978-0-618-06776-3.

Plamondon, Martin II, ed. (2001 and 2004) *Lewis and Clark Trail Maps: A Cartographic Reconstruction. Volumes II and III.* Pullman: Washington State University Press. ISBN: 978-0-87422-232-6

Randall, Willard Sterne (1993). *Thomas Jefferson: A Life.* New York: Holt. ISBN 978-0-0609-7617-0.

Ronda, James P. (2002). *Lewis and Clark among the Indians.* Lincoln: University of Nebraska Press. ISBN 978-0-8032-8990-1.

Russell, Steve F. (2007). *Lewis and Clark Across the Mountains: Mapping the Corps of Discovery in Idaho.* Boise: Idaho State Historical Society Press. ISBN 0-931406-16-1.

Sarasohn, David (2005). *Waiting for Lewis and Clark: The Bicentennial and the Changing West.* Portland: Oregon Historical Society. ISBN 978-0-8759-5295-6.

Schmidt, Thomas (2002). *National Geographic Guide to the Lewis and Clark Trail.* Washington, DC: National Geographic. ISBN 978-0-7922-6471-2.

Slaughter, Thomas P. (2003). *Exploring Lewis and Clark: Reflections on Men and Wilderness.* New York: Alfred A. Knopf. ISBN 978-0-375-40078-0.

Strong, Emory and Ruth. (1995). *Seeking Western Waters: The Lewis and Clark Trail from the Rockies to the Pacific.* Portland: Oregon Historical Society. ISBN 978-0-87595-245-1.

Tubbs, Stephenie Ambrose; Clay Straus Jenkinson (2003). *The Lewis and Clark Companion: An Encyclopedic Guide to the Voyage of Discovery.* New York: Henry Holt. ISBN 978-0-8050-6726-2.

# Follow the Route of Lewis and Clark

Thomas Jefferson, president of the young United States of America, was an optimist who also had a shrewd understanding of geopolitics. His young country was blocked from expanding to the north by Great Britain, to the south and west by Spain, and, after 1800, by France. The immense Louisiana Territory effectively blocked his vision of an America that would someday extend from sea to shining sea. Even before he learned, in 1803, that he would be able to buy Louisiana from France, be began his plans to explore what he knew must *someday* become American territory.

The daring enterprise was so important that he assigned its leadership to Meriwether Lewis, his own personal secretary. Lewis, in turn, recruited his former commanding officer, William Clark, to co-captain the expedition.

Leaving St. Louis on May 14, 1804, with thirty-four soldiers, hired voyagers, and Clark's slave, York, they traveled through the unexplored territory and beyond it, to the Pacific Ocean. Their exploits come alive today as cruise ships travel their route up and down the Snake and Columbia Rivers.

This book is designed to help passengers better understand what the Lewis and Clark expedition experienced during those momentous years of 1804–1806, but also to be able to see through vintage photographs and other images what the members of the Corps of Discovery saw before the rivers were changed forever by hydroelectric dams. It affords an opportunity to travel "in the wake of Lewis and Clark."